MARIJUANA EFFECTS

EXPOSING MARIJUANA'S SECRETS AND HOW IT
EFFECTS OUR MIND, BODY AND SOUL

JOSHUA CRABTREE

BETTER YOU ETC. PUBLISHING

INTRODUCTION

"Nature... she will hang the night stars so that I may walk abroad in the darkness without stumbling, and send word the wind over my footprints so that none may track me to my hurt: she will cleanse me in great waters, and with bitter herbs make me whole."

~ Oscar Wilde

It is time to let go of the stigma, myths, and misunderstandings that stand in the way of correct and efficient cannabis use.

Only if we bring it out into the open and understand it fully can we start becoming more discerning about the quality and methods that best suit our specific needs.

There are hundreds of Sativa strains and each type has specific benefits. Use the wrong strain and you will not get the results you were hoping for

There is no one type of marijuana user. Many users in today's cannabis culture are educated, diverse, and cultured, which is far from the antiquated stereotype of the typical stoner.

If you are already using cannabis and curious about how it is working for you, or considering using cannabis and need to be better informed, this practical, user-friendly book is going to be very helpful.

I hope you enjoy:)

1
___

CANNABIS' HAZY PAST

Cannabis sativa L. is perhaps one of the oldest plants grown by man, yet it has remained a contentious issue for the whole of the plant's history. Whether seen as a pariah or a panacea, this diverse plant has offered a mirror to medicine and paved the way in the past two decades for a variety of medical issues, ranging from analgesia to weight reduction, via the discovery of its numerous biochemical properties and the endocannabinoid system, through which many of the function of its constituent.

Cannabis Sativa, more often referred to as cannabis, was one of the first plants that humans cultivated. In China, archeological and historical studies reveal that cannabis was farmed for fibers as early as 4,000 B.C.I. This was the location where the earliest evidence of the usage of cannabis was discovered. The Chinese created paper, strings, ropes, and even textiles using the fibers that were extracted from the stems of cannabis plants. In the tomb of Emperor Wu,

who ruled the Han dynasty from 104 to 87 B.C., archaeolo-
gists discovered textiles and paper made from cannabis.

THE CHINESE also used the fruits of the cannabis plant as
food. These fruits range in size from 3 to 5 mm, are elliptic in
shape, are smooth, have a tough rind, and only contain a
single seed. During the Han period, archaeological excava-
tions uncovered the first traces of human interaction with
these seeds. At the beginning of the Christian era, with the
arrival of new cultures, cannabis ceased to be a significant
food in China; nevertheless, the seeds are still used for
manufacturing cooking oil in Nepal up to the present day.
This practice dates back to the beginning of the Christian
era.

THE PEN-TS'AO CHING, compiled in the first century of this
Era, was based on oral traditions passed down from the time
of Emperor Shen-Nung, who lived during the years 2.700
B.C., reports that the ancient Chinese used cannabis as a
medicine. This information can be found in the world's
oldest pharmacopeia, compiled in the first century of this
Era. Rheumatoid arthritis, discomfort, intestinal constipation, abnormalities of the female reproductive system,
malaria, and other conditions were some of the indications
for the use of cannabis. At the beginning of the Christian
period, Hua T'o considered the pioneer of Chinese surgery,
administered a combination made from the plant to
patients and wine to render them unconscious before
surgical procedures.

. . .

THE FACT that there are so few references to the usage of cannabis by the Greeks and Romans suggests that these cultures did not widely use it. However, at the beginning of the Christian era, there were two mentions of using the seed's juice for earache and driving worms and insects out of the ears. One of these references is found in the Book of Acts, while the other is in the Gospel of Mark.

FROM THE BEGINNING of the Christian era until the end of the 18th century

During this period, the usage of cannabis for medicinal purposes continued at a high level in India, and it later moved to the Middle East and Africa lands. Around 1000 A.D., renowned medical practitioners like Avicena included cannabis-related information in their respective medical encyclopedias. In Muslim scriptures, cannabis is used for various medicinal purposes, including as a laxative, a digestive aid, an anti-flatulent, "to clear the brain," and as a pain reliever for the ears. In 1464, Ibn al-Badri reported that the epileptic son of the caliph's chamberlain was treated with the plant's resin. He stated that: "it (cannabis) cured him completely; however, he became an addict who could not for a moment be without the drug." Ibn al-report Badri's was based on the fact that the plant's resin cured the epileptic son of the caliph.

DURING THIS PERIOD in European history, cannabis was grown solely to produce fibers. In 1150, Muslims began producing paper from cannabis, first in Spain and then Italy. Numerous publications created during this period about plants include descriptions of cannabis. These texts make it abundantly evident that the difference between male and female plants has been made since the middle of the 18th century (previously described in a Chinese ideogram at the beginning of the Christian Era). However, there are few instances when cannabis is used for medicinal purposes. The Europeans may have been aware of the plant's medicinal usage in Africa and the Middle East; however, they mistook it for opium because of its appearance.

CANNABIS and its Relation to Western Medicine in the 19th & 20th Centuries

Various records, some of which date back to the beginning of the 19th century, describe the use of cannabis by European doctors. These stories focus specifically on the use of seeds or homeopathic medicines. However, the practical introduction of cannabis into Western medicine did not occur until the middle of the 19th century. This was made possible by the works of Willian B. O'Shaughnessy, an Irish physician, and by the book written by Jacques-Joseph Moreau, a French psychiatrist. Both of these authors were active in Ireland.

O'SHAUGHNESSY, the Irish physician, spent some years serving the British in India, and it was in that nation that he had his first experience with cannabis. He began by reading the available literature on the plant, then described a variety of common preparations, assessed the plant's toxicity in animals, and conducted clinical trials on individuals suffering from various diseases. Finally, in the year 1839, he had the book titled "On the preparations of the Indian hemp, or gunjah" published. The opening line of this work presents a panorama of plant usage, including the following:

"THE NARCOTIC EFFECTS of Hemp are popularly known in the southern regions of Africa, South America, Turkey, Egypt, Middle East Asia, and India, as well as the adjacent territories of the Malay people, the Burmese people, and the Siamese people. Hemp, in all of these nations, is used in various ways by dissipated and depraved people as an easy agent of delightful intoxication. In addition, we discover that it is widely used in the traditional medicine of these cultures to treat a wide variety of diseases. However, neither as a stimulant nor a cure is often used in Western Europe. Neither of these uses is known to exist.

EMPEROR SHEN NUNG'S Influential Role in the Spread of Cannabis

It is said that the Chinese Emperor Shen Nung (also known as Chen Nung) discovered the medicinal benefits of Cannabis around the year 2700 BCE, along with those of ginseng and ephedra, which are two other essential components of traditional Chinese herbal medicine. The primary focus of attention was the efficacy of the substance as a treatment for rheumatism, menstruation disorders, gout, malaria, and, quite surprisingly, absent-mindedness. Author of *The Great Herbal*, Pen T'sao, is widely regarded as the "Father" of traditional Chinese medicine, a book that is still used today by practitioners of Traditional Chinese Medicine, even though it has most likely been changed from its original edition. He was also revered as the patron saint of all herbalists and apothecaries.

THE MYSTERIOUS EMPEROR Shen Neng of China began recommending marijuana tea to treat gout, rheumatism, malaria, and, interestingly enough, impaired memory as early as 2737 B.C. Quickly, the drug's use as a medicine expanded across Asia, the Middle East, and along the eastern coast of Africa.

AT THE END of the 19th century, when between 2% and 5% of the population of the United States was unknowingly addicted to morphine, a popular, secret ingredient in patent medicines, there was a shift in American attitudes toward marijuana. This shift occurred when marijuana was illegal in the United States. In 1906, the government passed the Pure Food and Drug Act, which established the Food and Drug Administration. This was done to reduce the number of people in the nation addicted to morphine. The regulation of chemical drugs was a significant departure from traditional American drug policy, even though it did not apply to marijuana and only placed the distribution of opium and morphine under the jurisdiction of medical professionals.

IN OCTOBER OF 2009, Attorney General Eric H. Holder Jr. gave the directive for federal prosecutors to stop pursuing lawsuits against patients who use medicinal marijuana, a move that signals a sweeping shift in the change in policy that proponents of drug reform are seeing as the first step toward legalization of medication in question According to the government's top lawyer, in the 14 states where specific rules are in effect, regarding the use of marijuana for medicinal purposes, federal prosecutors should exclusively concentrate on situations involving individuals who engage in higher-level drug trafficking, money laundering, or who utilize state laws as a cover.

THE SOCIAL ACCEPTANCE of Hashish Usage in Islam: Point and Counterpoint

Responsible political leaders saw the extensive use of hashish as a risk to society as the drug's popularity expanded and became more widely used. However, as long as the use of hashish was restricted to a subset of deviant Sufis, who constituted a relatively insignificant and less productive part of the population, the Ayyubid and Mamluk authorities showed little response to the practice.

GOVERNMENT OFFICIALS BECAME concerned when the drug started affecting all levels of society, including professionals and merchants. As a result, they made periodic attempts to limit or suppress drug use, not so much out of concern for moral or religious issues as they did for the state's safety.

DESPITE HAVING complete governmental and religious authority, they were never in a position to eliminate hashish use, even though they were successful in temporarily reducing consumption levels.

. . .

IN EGYPT, there were three new campaigns to get the substance declared illegal: In 1324, the governor of Cairo ordered confiscating and destroying wine and hashish supplies. According to al-Maqrizi7, the Ayyubid amir Sudun Shaikkuni gave the same commands as Ayyubid ruler Nizam fifty years later in 1376. Finally, in 1394, at the end of the century, Egyptian authorities in Cairo issued another edict that prohibited the use of hashish and ordered the removal of the plants. Even if these strenuous measures to limit or repress cannabis usage were unsuccessful, the fact that they were made suggests that the authorities believed the widespread use of cannabis was harmful to society. As Rosenthal states:

ISLAMIC SOCIETY DID NOT HAVE to fear the potential harm that hashish was able by prolonged use to inflict upon individual users. Its most crucial problem, which called for action, was the cumulative effect produced by large numbers of addicts. The periods when secular authorities tried openly and energetically to fight drug use were sporadic. They were not the result of a revival of religious fervor where doctrinal considerations determined the government's attitude. Instead, they reflected an acute fear that a potential social evil threatening the state's welfare might eventually get out of hand.

SOME KINGS WERE UNCONCERNED. For instance, the Sultan of Bagdad retired to Cairo in 1393 with his entourage, and while he was there, he was seen smoking hashish in public, which drew harsh condemnation from Egyptian governing circles. However, because of their stance and persistent efforts to outlaw cannabis growing, it is clear that Egyptian officials, in contrast to their counterparts in Bagdad, did not condone the use of the drug, even though its prevalence among the populace was high.

Application of Cannabis in Medicine

Cannabis has been used to treat medical conditions throughout all of these ages. However, the ancient manuscripts of Galen and Dioscorides did not account for all the medical applications of cannabis that Muslim doctors discovered. For example, al-Razi, a physician who practiced between the years 865 and 925, mentions using hemp leaves as a remedy for the ear. He also recommended using them to treat dandruff and dissolve flatulence.

He also discusses its capacity to treat epilepsy patients in a curative manner. In the year 1100 A.D., the German botanist Rumphius included a description of the Muslim usage of cannabis in his herbarium. Muslims used cannabis to cure asthma, gonorrhea, constipation, and as an antidote for poisoning. Other Arab doctors said that hashish was used to enhance the appetite (al-Badri, 1251) and generated a longing for sweets; other individuals characterized it as "a wonderful song to the sense of hearing."

Even though it 'opened the gates of desire,'[20] continued usage was thought to stifle an individual's willingness to engage in sexual activity. A pharmacopeia written in the 17th century by al-Intaqui recommends cannabis for treating many somatic disorders. The text also refers to the pleasure and lethargy caused by the substance.

. . .

Cannabis Use in Muslim Societies

Even though cannabis use was widespread in Muslim culture, it is difficult to identify the specific patterns of cannabis use that existed. Rosenthal asserts that "a considerable class separation was formed between proven addicts and the rest of the citizenry." [citation needed] People who indulged in hashish were stereotyped as being destitute and of low social standing because of their habit (harfasha).

The use of the substance "gives rise to a low social position (safalah) and a negative moral character (radhalah) " and "denies the existence of a well-ordered community." According to the data, the major users of hashish were the lower-class peasants who lacked education and the city workers who worked in cities, in addition to certain scholarly Sufis and authors.

Both factions began interacting and exchanging their mutual disdain for the corrupt system. Hashish was inexpensive and readily accessible to them; it could be found in the corner of every mosque. According to the assertions of one poet, "one ounce of hashish is more powerful than quarts of alcohol." Moreover, since the Prophet forbade drinking wine, using a substance that he did not mention and was simple to hide was considered a less shameful practice than drinking wine.

Hashish and the Muslim Intelligence Agency

The widespread use of cannabis in Islam between the 13th and 16th centuries was followed by a heated debate among the intelligentsia, which dwarfs the discussion among American intellectuals in the latter half of the 20th century. Many Islamic intellectuals, including jurists, historians, theologians, poets, and storytellers, debated the benefits and drawbacks of using the plant.

THE ORIGIN of the debate can be traced back to the fact that the holy Koran, which serves as the basis for Islamic legal doctrine, does not reference hashish. On the other hand, the Koran expressly prohibits using Khamr, which can be interpreted to mean both alcohol and other intoxicating substances.

THERE IS another proverb in the Koran that says, "Approach not prayers with a mind befogged not until you fully grasp everything that you say." (Sura Five verse 44) Because Muslims are required to pray five times a day at set intervals, the ban on praying while under the influence of intoxicants places significant restrictions on alcohol and other drugs.

AT THE TIME of the Prophet, khamr referred to wine; however, Muslim legal experts defined khamr as any intoxication that befogs the intellect over the three centuries that followed Mahomet's death. In other words, wine was not the only thing considered to fall under this category. "The term khamr is derived from the verb khamara, which means to hide or conceal, and communicates the sense of a drug that covers up the mind." However, the interpretation provided by the legal specialists did not match the common use, which continued to associate khamr with wine alone.

THE PROHIBITION on drinking fermented drinks did not automatically extend to the use of hashish in the eyes of many Moslems. Despite this debate, three of the four schools of Islamic law, Maliki, Shafi'i, and Hanbali, defined hashish as an intoxicant and eventually made it illegal for any real Sunni Muslim believer to consume it.

Hemp & Flax in Colonial America

Colonial planters enthusiastically praised the potential of Hemp. Col. William Byrd II referred to the cultivation of this plant as "the Darling of all my Projects." Robert Beverley made the prognostication that the plant "will be of the utmost concern to us." Thomas Jefferson directed that "an acre of the best ground" at his Poplar Forest estate be kept for a permanent patch of the stuff. However, the "Indian weed" prevalent in the 18th century and was responsible for so many people in the United States making or breaking their fortunes was not the object of their passion. This was a weed of a different kind that would gather healthy shares of acclaim and condemnation in the same way.

ALTHOUGH COLONIAL AMERICANS were familiar with hemp, they did not do so for the same reason that the plant would be in the news more than two centuries later. It is not the first time cannabis has captivated the country's attention, and today's discussion, which centers on the legalization of marijuana, is not the first time this argument has taken place. The fact that cannabis might get people high was only a side effect for thousands of people living in the United States in the 18th century, ranging from poor and middle-class farmers to wealthy plantation owners like Byrd, Beverley, and Jefferson. They were more interested in a quality they regarded as much more valued.

BECAUSE OF THEIR remarkable tensile and abrasion resistance, hemp fibers were a valuable commodity in times when scientific advancements prevented them from being superseded.

ONE OF THE first plants that were grown by humans was hemp. Hemp rope may have been used at least as far back as 5,000 years ago when it was imprinted on ancient Chinese ceramics and may have been used for longer. The myriad uses of hemp, including its ability to be made into thread, cordage, fabric, paper, food, and, yes, intoxicating substances, are to thank for the longevity of this connection.

THE MODERN HISTORY of Cannabis in The United States

Over the past 20 years, most Blue States and a few Red States have changed their laws to make cannabis legal for medical or recreational use. This is now known as the modern history of cannabis in the United States. But unfortunately, only Red states haven't changed their laws about cannabis yet. Finally, people in the Deep South and the Wild West are slowly coming to the idea that cannabis can save their states from financial ruin and help people get better in these challenging times.

. . .

AT THE FEDERAL LEVEL, marijuana is listed as a drug that could be harmful and lead to addiction, so states that legalize it could have different effects. However, regarding future laws, the change in the political climate and who holds office in the Senate will soon make it possible to de-schedule cannabis or at least allow favorable banking laws. This will allow free trade and make banks friendlier.

CURRENTLY, as of 2022, 38 states and Washington, D.C., have legalized selling medical marijuana. Legalization in conservative states, in particular, puts more pressure on federal lawmakers from those states to consider changes like the SAFE Banking Act, which the U.S. House of Representatives passed in 2019.

IN THE MEANTIME, the coronavirus pandemic has hurt state budgets and led more states to consider legalizing marijuana to create jobs, boost the economy, and bring in much-needed tax money.

THESE BUDGET PROBLEMS are one reason states from the Mid-Atlantic (New York and New Jersey) to the Southwest (New Mexico) are trying to legalize M.J. for recreational use.

THESE FINANCIAL WORRIES could also make lawmakers in the four states expected to look at medical marijuana laws this year act. Bills are being considered in Alabama, Kentucky, and South Carolina, and supporters of the policy are optimistic about Kansas, even though two medical marijuana bills introduced in that state's legislature last year died in committee.

The Ever-Changing Laws on Cannabis

During the Great Depression, when there was a lot of unemployment and social unrest, people became angry at Mexican immigrants and afraid of the "evil weed." By 1931, cannabis was illegal in 29 states, which was in line with how all drugs were seen during the Prohibition era.

The Marijuana Tax Act of 1937 was the first law in the United States that made marijuana illegal everywhere. The Act put an excise tax on the sale, possession, or transfer of all hemp products. This made it illegal to use the plant for anything other than industrial purposes.

As part of the "War on Drugs," President Richard Nixon signed the Controlled Substances Act of 1970 into law. This law eliminated the Marijuana Tax Act and put marijuana on the same list as heroin, L.S.D., and ecstasy.

In 1972, a report called "Marijuana: A Signal of Misunderstanding" was released by the National Commission on Marijuana and Drug Abuse, also known as the Shafer Commission. The report called for "partial prohibition" and less harsh punishments for people who have small amounts of marijuana on their person. However, Nixon and other government officials ignored the report.

THE COMPASSIONATE USE Act of 1996 made California the first state to let people with severe or long-term illnesses use marijuana as medicine. In addition, the use of cannabis for limited medical purposes is now legal in Washington, D.C., 38 states, and the U.S. territories of Guam and Puerto Rico.

"JUST SAY NO"

In 1982, the "Just Say No" movement began. When Nancy Reagan was on a speaking tour and went to an elementary school as part of that tour, the phrase started to be used. During the visit, she answered the students' questions. The Reagan Foundation thinks back to that time.

SHE REMEMBERED that a little girl raised her hand and asked, "Mrs. Reagan, what do you do if someone offers you drugs?" "Well, you just say "no," I said."

THIS IS where it all began.

IN THE EARLY and middle 1980s, Nancy Reagan went on a press tour to help the fight against drugs. She spoke dozens of times about the issue that was important to her. In 1984 alone, she went to 110 places and gave 14 speeches against drugs.

·   ·   ·

To stop young people from using drugs and alcohol, she went to 65 cities in 33 states and nine other countries. According to the Reagan Foundation, she also invited the spouses of 24 heads of state to a three-day anti-drug forum in the United States to bring more attention to the issue worldwide.

In 1986, President Reagan made the first "Just Say No to Drugs Week" official by signing a proclamation.

In September 1986, when Mrs. Reagan was helping with the campaign, she gave a televised speech to the whole country. Her speech was mostly about her time traveling for her anti-drug campaign and what she thought was the best way to help the anti-drug movement move forward.

She said, "For the past five years, I've been traveling across the country to learn and listen... One of the most encouraging things I've seen is that people are becoming more aware of how bad and dangerous drug abuse is to our society. ... You can't just do nothing. For the sake of our children, we want you to help us make it clear that we don't accept drug use. I beg you to be firm and unwavering in your fight against drugs."

During the speech, she also said the most famous line from the movement: "Say "yes" to your life." And just say "no" when it comes to drugs and alcohol."

. . .

THE MOVEMENT WAS COVERED by news outlets all over the country, and famous people from pop culture were asked to talk about the problem. Whitney Houston, David Hasselhoff, Kareem Abdul-Jabbar, and Arnold Schwarzenegger were among the well-known people who joined Nancy Reagan in "Just Say No" campaigns.

BY 1988, there were more than 12,000 "Just Say No" clubs all over the country and the world. Many of these clubs and groups are still going strong.

SIMILARLY, the Drug Abuse Resistance Education (D.A.R.E.) program and the "Just Say No" campaign were used to get people to stop using drugs.

WAR ON DRUGS

Since the 1970s, the U.S. has fought illegal drug usage through increasing sanctions, enforcement, and imprisonment. This has come to be known as the War on Drugs.

IN JUNE 1971, Nixon proclaimed drug misuse "public enemy number one" and boosted money for drug-control organizations and treatment programs. In 1973, the Office for Drug Abuse Law Enforcement, the Bureau of Narcotics and Dangerous Drugs, and the Office of Narcotics Intelligence merged to become the Drug Enforcement Administration.

. . .

BEFORE RONALD REAGAN'S 1981 administration, the War on Drugs was only a modest part of federal law enforcement. Reagan's concentration on criminal punishment over treatment led to a significant rise in nonviolent drug offense incarcerations, from 50,000 in 1980 to 400,000 in 1997. Nancy Reagan's "Just Say No" program educated students about the hazards of drug usage in 1984. In many respects, the crack epidemic of the early 1980s drove the growth of the War on Drugs since it increased worry about drug usage and boosted Reagan's hard-line approach to drugs. Anti-Drug Abuse Act of 1986 gave $1.7 billion to the War on Drugs and set "mandatory minimum" prison penalties for drug crimes. Possession of five grams of crack led to a five-year sentence, whereas 500 grams of powder cocaine triggered that same exact term. Mandatory minimums led to disproportionate imprisonment rates for nonviolent Black drug offenders and claims from many that the War on Drugs was a racist movement entirely.

CONCERNS REGARDING THE WAR ON DRUGS' efficacy and the racial imbalance of its sentences led to diminished popular support in the early 21st century. In response, new measures were adopted, such as the legalization of recreational marijuana in more states and the Fair Sentencing Act of 2010, which dropped the crack-to-powder ratio for minimum terms from 100-to-1 to 18-to-1. In addition, the 2018 prison reform law decreased crack cocaine punishments. The War on Drugs is still being fought, albeit less intensely than in the 1980s.

2

THE PLANT IN ALL ITS GLORIOUS FORMS

Hundreds. Thousands. It's hard to say how many different types of cannabis there are. Why? There are always new strains of cannabis being made. Most large strain databases have websites that list more than 3,600 different kinds of cannabis. On the other hand, the vast majority of these varieties are small cannabis strains that most people have never heard of. Cannabis experts say there are probably more than 700 different strains, and the rest may be variations of these 700.

That's a big difference. Here's what makes the difference. Cannabis breeds a lot like people do (well, not that way.) Cannabis plants are usually either male or female. So, when two plants are bred together, the seeds will have genetic information from both the male (the father plant) and the female (the mother plant), just like people do.

So, different cannabis plants can have a lot of different genes. It also makes it easy to choose plants with desirable traits and cross-breed them to create a new plant with the best of both worlds. Once breeders have stabilized a unique mix of cannabis plants, they call it a new cultivar or strain.

Then, that "strain" is named and sold as a unique kind of cannabis, like Blue Dream or Cat Piss.

Or like the Blue Cookies strain, for example. Girl Scout Cookies and Blueberry, two well-known flavors, gave birth to the hybrid. Blue Cookies can go on the market as their unique strain after it has been stabilized for maybe a few generations. So, if you bought Blue Cookies seeds, you would get seeds from a Blue Cookies plant that was crossed with another Blue Cookies plant. If you wanted a clone, you would get one cut from a Blue Cookies plant. Some strains, like Blue Cookies, are well-known enough to get the general public's attention. Some are small-scale local legends grown by people in their backyards or basements.

However, this isn't the only way that these plants are grown. People have been crossing, picking, and stabilizing crops for thousands of years. As a result, there may be more than 3,600 known types of cannabis plants. There are also more than 3,000 registered types of tulips and more than 10,000 types of wine grapes. We make new ones to protect them from pests, make them taste better, help them deal with drought, and so on.

Silly Spinach... The Devil's Lettuce is... Giggle Bush – There are hundreds of traditional ways to talk about cannabis that differ from one place to the next. Green, ganja, and weed are all well-known names for sticky green buds in many English-speaking parts of the world. However, how do these names compare in other countries and cultures?

Now that it's safe to travel again, it might be nice to know what the locals call cannabis. Is a joint still a joint in Italy? Does "grass" translate to people over in France? Is there a different word for ganja in Polish?

If you're planning on traveling and you're not quite sure how to talk about weed in new places, don't worry. Here are some of the names for cannabis in different parts of the world. Next time you're headed out on your next traveling adventure, just turn to this page and you'll be equipped with the locals' language for weed.

Australia

Most of the common Western words for cannabis are known in Australia, like "grass" and "weed." However, "hooch" is what the older people in Australia call it. This may seem a little strange initially because in other parts of the world, "hooch" is the name for homemade alcohol that can make an elephant fall over with just one sip. However, "hooch" is slang for your favorite smoke in Australia.

Some parts of Australia have part-time smokers who call cannabis "choof." This word refers to the plant and the act of smoking it, as in "meet me outside later for a quick choof."

Brazil

The primary language in Brazil is Portuguese, and the word for marijuana in Portuguese is "maconha" (pron. maconya). In the same way, "erva" means "herb," and "beck" is slang for "joint."

China

"Ma" or "Dama" are ancient Mandarin words for cannabis that are still used today. Hemp is grown and used in China, even though cannabis is against the law. Even modern medical writings use terms like "mafen," "mahua," and "mabo." Which describes parts of the cannabis plant that have different amounts of cannabinoids?

Denmark

Cannabis is called "tjald" here. This word has been used since the 1970s when the Copenhagen rock band Gasolin' came up with it so they could talk about cannabis without people understanding them. The story goes that they saw a ship in the harbor of Copenhagen called Tjaldur, which in

Faroese means "oystercatcher." So they thought "Tjald" would be a good code name for marijuana. Hendrix influenced the four-piece; however, they didn't cover Jimi's song "Voodoo Tjald," which would have been much cooler.

Germany

In Germany, people say "Gras" when they talk about marijuana. But, like another German name, "Hasch," it's easy to say and remember. "Hasch Kekse" refers to foods with secret ingredients, like brownies or cookies. It sounds a lot like words we all know.

Netherlands

If you ever decide to go to Amsterdam because of its cannabis culture, don't worry too much about not being able to speak the language. You only need to know one word – "Wiet," which looks like "weed," sounds like "weed," and I'll wager it even smells like weed, too.

South Africa

The most common word for cannabis in South Africa is "Dagga." This is an Afrikaans word for the plant that dates back to the 1600s. However, don't say it the way it looks. The double "g" in "dagga" should be pronounced more like the "ch" in "loch." In South Africa, there is even a Dagga Party, which sounds like a fun night out however is a political party that wants to make their favorite plant legal. It's also called a "zol," which gave us this great tune when we were in lockdown.

France

"La beuh" is the French word for "bud," and "Petard" is the word for a joint in French. The cannabis resin is sometimes called "Le Shit." Ask for "Le Shit" if you want the good stuff; however, how do you tell someone it's really good? "Le Shit is Le Shit"?

Spain

In Spain, the most common names for cannabis are "Mota" and "Hierba." Hierba is the word for "herb," which is pretty self-explanatory. Mota is "mote," a speck or small amount of cannabis for personal use. So before your afternoon nap, have a mota. You can be sure that these words will also help you get by in Mexico.

Italy

"Erba" is easy to remember when you're in Rome; however, "Spinello" is another Italian word for cannabis. It means "reefer" in English; however, it means a joint in Italy. So, does anyone want a Gelat Spinello? OG?

Egypt

In Egypt, cannabis is called "bango," a pretty cool name. It means "weed," Bedouin people in the Sinai Peninsula and some poor people in cities smoke it (probably after Bingo) because it's easy to grow and cheaper than hashish, which is hard to grow. It sounds like the word that Hindus and Indians use for marijuana.

India

The word "Bhang" in Sanskrit may be the oldest word for marijuana. However, it is more likely to mean seeds and leaves in India. Natives make a paste from the buds, leaves, and flowers of the marijuana plant that can be eaten. This paste is added to drinks like bhang lassi and bhang thandai, milkshake-like drinks made with cannabis plant extracts that have been ground up.

Cannabis Varies in Potency

Cannabis, also known as marijuana, is used by many people worldwide; however, not many know that it has become stronger over time. Since the 1970s, cannabis has changed a lot. New ways of making marijuana, like hydroponic cultivation, have made tetrahydrocannabinol (THC), the most psychoactive chemical in marijuana, stronger and worse for your health. Because cannabis is linked to health problems, including mental health problems, it is essential to know how strong it is.

Most of the time, the amount of THC in a sample of cannabis is used to measure how strong it is. However, in 2004, the European Monitoring Centre for Drugs and Drug Addiction (EMCDDA) did one of the most thorough studies. It found that there had been a slight increase in the overall potency of cannabis, which may be due to the use of intensive indoor cultivation methods. The study's authors did say, though, that THC content varied a lot.

Percentage of THC

If you use cannabis, you probably know about THC, the most well-known psychoactive cannabinoid found naturally in cannabis. However, if you've ever bought cannabis from a dispensary, you've probably also noticed that the amount of THC in different products varies significantly.

Many people who use cannabis find it hard to understand what a product's THC percentage means, how different levels of THC will affect them, and what to look for when it comes to THC content.

What Do I Need to Look For?

Most of the time, products with a higher THC percentage will have a stronger, more potent effect. Most cannabis flowers have between 15 and 25 percent THC. The biological limit for THC percentage is 35%, so it is possible, though rare, to find a flower with more than 25% THC. Therefore, you can expect anything over 25 percent to be very strong.

If you don't know what the right amount of THC is for you, these guidelines can help you figure it out.

Most of the time, flower with a total THC content of 7 to 11.99% (about 70 to 119.99mg of THC per gram) has mild psychoactive effects. This is a lower-than-average amount of THC; however, it's good for people who want a mild high.

Medium-strength flower has a total THC content of between 12 and 16.99 percent, about 120 to 169.99mg of THC per gram. This is a little less THC than average; however, it still makes you feel pretty high.

High-potency flower has a total amount of THC between 17 and 20%, or about 170 to 200 mg of THC per gram. Most flowers at a dispensary will have a THC level in this range, and the effects will be stronger.

What's the THC limit?

When it comes to the amount of THC, it's usually up to the customer and how comfortable they are with cannabis products. If someone takes more THC than they are used to, especially if they are new to cannabis, they may feel harmful effects. The best way to figure out how much THC you like and can handle is to start small and gradually add more over time. This gives you a chance to get used to the product and learn more about how it works for you.

However, the THC percentage isn't the only thing that affects a product's strength; it can be hard to tell how a product will affect you based on its THC percentage alone. First, each cannabis user may react differently to the same strains or products, and two strains with the same amount of THC can give the same person two very different highs.

The effects of a strain or product can differ depending on how it is used, what kind of strain it is, and what kind of terpenes it has. Therefore, in addition to the THC percentage, it's essential to pay attention to the strain's terpene profile, which often shows the strain's effects (e.g., whether the strain is more energizing or sedative). Terpenes don't directly affect how strong a strain is; however, the different effects can make for very different experiences.

Concentrates vs. Flowers

The amount of THC in different kinds of cannabis products varies. Cannabis will have a higher percentage of THC and, as a result, a stronger effect. This makes them a popular choice among people who have used cannabis before.

Concentrates can have anywhere from 50 to 90 percent THC, while flower only has about 15 to 25 percent. This is because the concentrate is mostly extracted cannabinoids and has no plant material. So, in the end, one gram of concentrate will have much more THC than one gram of flower, making it much more potent.

THC percentage is an important metric that shows a product's strength and effectiveness. Knowing how much THC is in a product can help you predict how it will affect you. Just remember the other parts of the strain and how they affect you as well.

Hashish and Marijuana

Hash is made by taking the plant parts off of female cannabis plants and collecting the trichomes from the tops of the plants. The THC content is much higher in the flower heads than in any other part of the plant. This is because the flower heads have the most trichomes, which makes them the most potent. Usually, the most THC found in a typical strain of marijuana is between 25% and 35%. The amount of THC in hashish, on the other hand, can range from 20% to 60%. Since there is more THC in Hash, you need much less of it to get high. Users also have to choose what kind of high they want since different strains of marijuana have different effects.

People know that "young" hashish from early plants has a higher ratio of THC to CBD, making people feel more buzzed and "racy." If the hash were cured for less time before selling, the user would also get high because less THC has been turned into CBN. It's important to note that Sativas will have a stronger effect than Indicas after going through the process of making hash.

Hash comes in two main types: dry-sift and hand-rubbed. Many different factors can show whether the hash is good or bad. Good dry-sifted hash should look from light yellow to reddish brown, and the color should be the same throughout. It shouldn't be too dry because that means it wasn't stored well. Instead, it should be soft and crumbly, with an oily, sticky feel. It can be hard, but it should soften if you touch it.

Hash that is rubbed by hand should be dark brown to black. It shouldn't look green because that would mean there is still too much plant matter inside. Hashish that has been rubbed by hand should be dense and not too sticky. Stickiness is a sign that extra oils and impurities have been added.

Flavor and smell can tell you if there are contaminants in the food. Also, it should be checked for mold because plant moisture can get trapped inside and grow mold if it isn't processed correctly. The "Bubble test" is a tried-and-true way to test if the hash's good and strong. You must put a piece of hash before a flame to do this. If the hash is good, it will bubble; if it is very good, it will catch fire quickly and burn with a clean flame.

If the test shows that the hash is black, other things were burned along with the resin. If the hash doesn't bubble, it's probably not very good. "It's not worth the trouble if it doesn't bubble."

The Side Effects of Marijuana and Hashish

Most national surveys on the use and abuse of drugs group marijuana and hashish abuse together. For example, the 2015 National Survey on Drug Use and Health

(NSDUH), released by the National Institute on Drug Abuse (NIDA), found that almost 45 percent of Americans aged 12 and up said they had tried either marijuana or hashish at some point in their lives. It can be hard to know how many people specifically use hashish or marijuana; however, marijuana use is probably more common in the US, while hashish may be more common in the Middle East, where it is often trafficked.

Teenagers and young adults often use too much marijuana. According to a national survey by NIDA for Teens in 2013, one out of every seven teens said they had used marijuana in the month before the survey.

Federally, marijuana and hashish are illegal in the United States. The DEA considers cannabis a Schedule I controlled substance with no known medical uses. On a local level, however, most states are working to legalize marijuana, if they haven't already, so it can be used as medicine or even for fun. Marijuana may help with pain and anxiety, make you hungry, and stop you from getting sick; however, more research is needed to prove these claims.

How marijuana and hashish affect the body and brain

Since marijuana and hashish contain THC, they have the same effects on the brain and body. Cannabis gives people a mellow "high" that makes them feel relaxed, happy, unmotivated, unable to control their bodies, hungry, forgetful, and confused about time and senses. However, long-term marijuana or hashish use can cause problems with the lungs and breathing, an irregular heart rate, a decline in thinking skills, and a change in the way the brain grows and develops in younger people.

You may become dependent if you use marijuana or hashish often and for a long time. When the drug leaves the body, it can cause anxiety, depression, irritability, trouble sleeping, restlessness, cravings, a loss of appetite, problems thinking and feeling, and mood changes. These unpleasant withdrawal symptoms can make it addicting. The National Institute on Drug Abuse (NIDA) says that as many as one-third of regular marijuana users may have problems with addiction.

Know your Cannabis Strain

Plant materials, or dendrology for forestry students, is one of the first classes that horticulture students take. Why? Pretty simple. Choosing plants is hard if you don't know what they are and what they'll do in the landscape. Of course, the classic example is a big tree or bush planted in a tight spot and grows so big that it eats a whole house. However, it's not hard to find cases where a homeowner or landscaper didn't know what kind of plant they were dealing with. There are many ways to say that plants are important. However, good health is one of the most important ones.

When you go to a dispensary, there are so many products and strains to choose from that it can be hard to know where to start. Because of marketing and new ways of breeding cannabis, there are a lot of different strains on the shelf. There's a lot of information, so it's hard to know what to buy when you're just starting. Let's take a closer look at the different types of marijuana strains so that you can make smart choices as a new medical marijuana user.

What do "strains" of marijuana mean?

Strains are different kinds of the same type of plant. In the culture of marijuana, "strains" are "different breeds of cannabis" bred for specific traits like the smell, cannabinoid and terpene profiles, and mental and physical effects. Cannabinoids are chemical compounds found in marijuana, and you can learn more about them here.

Most strain names are made for marketing, to hint at the strain, or to show where it came from. For example, the words "tangy" and "orange" are used to describe strains that smell like citrus fruits, while the word "diesel" is used to describe strains that smell like gasoline. On the other hand, Afghan Kush and Acapulco Gold tell you where the strain comes from.

Growers and cultivators of marijuana are always coming up with new strains and putting them on the market. They also cross-breed strains to make new strains with traits from both parents. For example, growers would choose two strains (one male and one female) that both contained the cannabinoid cannabigerol (CBG) and breed them to make a strain with a lot of CBG.

The male and female plants are then put close to each other so that the male plant can pollinate the female plant. Next, the female plant makes seeds that have traits from both the male and female plants. Then, the breeders take the seeds and do something called "backcrossing," when the new strain is bred with itself or with a parent to strengthen it. Backcrossing might need to be done more than once to get the desired result. Let's look at some of the ways that strains are different.

Is there a difference between THC and CBD?

The two most common cannabinoids, tetrahydrocannabinol (THC) and cannabidiol (CBD), are found in different amounts in different strains. THC and CBD are both psychoactive, which may come as a surprise. This means that they both affect the brain. THC, on the other hand, makes you feel high, while CBD does not. THC is what gives marijuana its "high" and can change how people see things. CBD can stop this high feeling and is well-known for its medical benefits. Because of this, many people who use medical marijuana choose strains with more CBD than THC to avoid getting high.

Does it matter whether a plant is Sativa or Indica?

In the past, people thought that indicas were more soothing while sativas were more uplifting and energizing. It's important to know that putting strains into categories like Indica, Sativa, or hybrid is outdated and doesn't give an accurate idea of what to expect from them. This is because strains have been crossed with each other so much that there are no longer any pure "indicas" or "sativas."

On the other hand, science has started to change how the business world groups marijuana products. Type I, Type II, and Type III are the names given to these important groups. In short, Type I has more THC than CBD, Type II has an equal amount of CBD and THC, and Type III has more CBD than THC. With these more useful categories, people can choose the kind that best fits their needs.

Most Popular Marijuana Strains

Even though there are a lot of different kinds of marijuana, some of them have become very popular because of how they taste, smell, and make people feel. Some might even say that these well-known strains are legendary. Let's check them out.

Strain 1: Amnesia Haze

People say that Amnesia Haze is a strain that gives you energy and makes you feel good. It has citrusy, lemony, earthy flavors and terpene geraniol. This strain has won the Cannabis Cup and is said to make people happier and give them more energy. Because it gives you energy, it's a good choice for social events and activities like hiking and working out.

Strain 2: Blue Dream

Blue Dream smells and tastes like berries and is sweeter.

It's known for making people feel calmer and sharper simultaneously. Some have noted that Blue Dream effects last longer, are more balanced, and have a more pleasant smell. This strain goes well with yoga, watching a movie, and hanging out with friends at dinner parties. It's also an excellent choice for people just starting to grow their plants at home.

Strain 3: Bruce Banner

This strain may sound familiar to you because it was named after the Hulk's alter ego. Bruce Banner makes people feel happy, creative, and full of energy while also calming them down. This strain tastes citrusy and earthy, with a hint of diesel. It has limonene and is a good strain for the day. It goes well with things like creative projects and trips outside. Because it has a lot of THC, it is also often used to treat pain.

Strain 4: Durban Poison

Durban Poison comes from South Africa. It is an award-winning strain that has become popular for making people feel creative, energetic, and happy. This strain could also give a good mix of a relaxing body high and an alert head high. It can smell sweet like orange or lemon or spicy like anise. It's good to smoke during the day, and it goes well with activities that require focus, like hiking, surfing, or making art.

Strain 5: Girl Scout Cookies

Girl Scout Cookies is a cross between Durban Poison and OG Kush. It is known for giving people a body high that makes them feel happy and relaxed. This strain, which has won awards, smells and tastes sweet and spicy and is known to help people lose weight. It goes best with evening activities like relaxing on the couch, watching TV, playing video games, or hanging out with friends.

6: The Northern Lights

Northern Lights is a sweet, earthy, and energizing strain that could make your body numb, happy, and high. Find a comfortable place to watch the Northern Lights. You could curl up on the couch and watch a lot of movies. You might want to exercise as little as possible and have some snacks if you get hungry.

Strain 7: OG Kush

Because of how strong it is and how good it smells and tastes, OG Kush might be the most popular strain. OG Kush smells like citrus and spices and is thought to be strong. This strong strain has physical and mental effects, like making you more aware of your surroundings, making you feel happy, and giving you a sense of stability. Based on these effects, it seems like OG Kush goes well with things like playing games, doing yoga, or going to a party.

Strain 8: Sour Diesel

Sour Diesel is known for having effects on the brain and having a taste and smell that are both herbal and almost chemical. Even though the strains have a strong flavor that could be overwhelming, their effects are euphoric, energetic, and make you think. This strain can make you talkative when you're around other people; however, it's also great for quiet study time or self-reflection, like meditation or writing in a journal.

Strain 9: Super Silver Haze

Super Silver Haze has won several High Times Cannabis Cups and gives a body high that is energizing and uplifting. Super Silver Haze has tastes that are spicy, citrusy, and skunky. Because it makes you feel energized, this strain is good to use during more active daytime activities like cycling, working out, or hiking. Some people also find that the body high helps with pains and aches.

10: The White Widow

White Widow was grown by Scott Blakey. It smells like pine, sandalwood, and other herbs and spices from the earth. It is said to make people feel very energized, stimulated, and happy. White Widow is a good choice for group activities like dancing, picnics, and even arts and crafts.

Even though these ten strains are popular, others like Jack Herer, Super Lemon Haze, and AK-47 could also qualify. However, let's move on to the exotic strains, which are more exciting and harder to find.

Rare Strains of Weed

Many serious marijuana users go out of their way to find rarer strains. These strains have unique tastes, smells, looks, and often strong effects. For example, Snowcap is thought to be an exotic strain because it tastes very much like menthol.

Pinkman Goo, known for its pink and purple color, is one of the most unusual and interesting strains. The story goes that a woman found the seeds for this strain behind an appliance in her kitchen. This plant's resin is a pinkish substance that looks like "goo."

Each strain can yield its unique effects, so finding the best can truly be a personal journey that has more to do with you and what you want to experience. Use the link below to take an interactive quiz to find the strain that best suits your needs.

https://silver-therapeutics.com/cannabis-strains-101/

3

MIND - BODY - SOUL

The Endocannabinoid System
The immune system, the respiratory system, the vascular system, the nervous system, and the endocannabinoid system are all parts of every person. The endocannabinoid system (ECS), like these other, better-known systems, is an integral part of how our bodies work. Its main job is to help keep our biological systems in a state of homeostasis, which means they are in a natural balance.

IT WORKS like a modulator that reacts to changes inside and outside the body that would otherwise cause it to act strangely. For example, it tells some systems to slow down when they are moving too quickly and speed up when they are moving too slowly. As a result, you can help strengthen and protect your ECS, just like you can help the other systems in your body.

HOW DOES the body's system of cannabinoids work?

The ECS is the largest group of neurotransmitters in your body and comprises a complicated web of connections. It is made up of CB1 and CB2 cannabinoid receptors. Our brain and spinal cord, which are part of our central nervous system, have CB1 receptors. Our muscles, limbs, skin, and other organ structures are all connected to our peripheral nervous system through the CB2 receptors. Endogenous cannabinoids, which are made by the body, stimulate these receptors.

ANANDAMIDE (AEA) and 2-arachidonoylglycerol are the two types of endocannabinoids that our bodies make (2-ag). When endocannabinoids attach to their receptors, they send a signal that helps control things like inflammation, sleep, and even how neurons talk to each other.

ENDOCANNABINOID DEFICIENCY

Endocannabinoids only show up when they are needed. Therefore, after sending signals through cannabinoid receptors, the ECS uses fatty acid amide hydrolase (FAAH) and monoacylglycerol lipase to break down molecules (MAGL). These enzymes break down the endocannabinoid molecules until they are needed again.

RESEARCH SHOWS that in some cases, the ECS might not work as it should for some people. For example, Endocannabinoid deficiency can happen because of your diet, because you don't have enough cannabinoid receptors, or because you have too many metabolic enzymes. Even though we are still studying and trying to fully understand the ECS, there are some things you can do to help it work better and improve your health and well-being.

Cannabis and Cannabinoids

Cannabinoids, the most important part of the ancient medicinal plant Cannabis sativa (marijuana), have biological effects mediated by cannabinoid receptors 1 (CB1R) and 2. The CB1R is the most common subtype in the central nervous system (CNS). Therefore, it has gotten much attention as a possible way to treat neuropsychological disorders and neurodegenerative diseases, among other diseases.

Cannabinoids also change how signals are sent and strongly affect peripheral sites. However, even though cannabinoids could be used as medicine, their ability to make people feel high has made it hard for doctors to use them. In this review, we gave a brief overview of what we know about cannabinoids and the endocannabinoid system, with a focus on the CB1R and the CNS and a focus on recent advances in the field.

We want to figure out what roles cannabinoid receptors might play in regulating signaling pathways and in several pathophysiological conditions. We think that the adverse effects of cannabinoids hide their therapeutic value. Here, we discuss other ways to use cannabinoids for their therapeutic value.

4

———

CANNABIS FOR MOOD

Key takeaway: With the pandemics of stress, anxiety, and depression heading the charts of severe disease, causing chronic cardiac, neurological, autoimmune, and a range of other issues if left untreated, using a gentle herb to manage the early stages makes more sense.

EVERY PART of our lives is affected by how we feel. If you are sad, worried, or depressed, you may find yourself spending less time with friends and family. You might start to avoid going out with people. Whether you have a bad mood because of a physical problem or because of a mental health problem like anxiety or depression, cannabis may be able to help. Here are some of the ways that pot can make you feel better.

PAIN RELIEF with cannabis is becoming more and more popular. When the cannabinoids interact with your cannabinoid receptors, they can help to dull the signals sent to the brain, giving you much-needed relief.

If you have anxiety, depression, or PTSD, cannabis can also help improve your mood. These mental health problems affect your mood, just like pain does. Some strains of marijuana can help you feel less anxious and feel better all around. As the cannabinoids interact with your cannabinoid receptors, they can also help to get your brain to make more dopamine.

Even though cannabis is an excellent way to help improve your mood, you must ensure you get the correct dose. If you take too much, especially a THC strain, you might get the opposite of what you want. For example, if you use weed to deal with anxiety, too much THC can worsen your symptoms instead of making you feel better.

Starting small is one of the best ways to find the correct dose. Even 1mg of THC is enough to start. Then, boost your dose slowly until you start feeling the desired effects. You might find it helpful to write down the strain you are using and how it makes you feel in a journal.

Disclaimer on using the High marijuana

Marijuana has chemicals that change the way your brain and body work. It can be addicting and might be bad for some people's health. When you use marijuana, these things can happen:

. . .

Getting "High" Is Possible.

This is why most people try pot. The main psychoactive ingredient, THC, makes the part of your brain that responds to pleasure, like food and sex, work harder. That makes a dopamine chemical, which makes you feel happy and calm.

If you vape or smoke weed, the THC could get into your bloodstream quickly enough for you to feel high in seconds or minutes. The THC level usually peaks in about 30 minutes, and its effects can last anywhere from 1 to 3 hours. If you drink or eat pot, it could take a long time to feel normal again. You might not always know how potent the marijuana you buy for fun is. Most medical marijuana is the same way.

It might be **bad for your mind.**

Not everyone has a good time when they use marijuana. It can often make you worried, scared, panicky, or paranoid. Using marijuana could make you more likely to get clinical depression or worsen the symptoms of any mental illness you already have. Scientists still don't know for sure why. High doses can make you feel paranoid or hallucinate.

Your thinking might get **messed up.**

Marijuana can cloud your senses and judgment. The effects can differ depending on how strong the pot was, how it was taken, and how much marijuana you've used. It could:

. . .

•Heighten your senses (colors might seem brighter, and sounds might seem louder)
•Change your perception of time
•Hurt your motor skills and make driving more dangerous
•Lower your guard so you can try risky sex or other things

If you get too high, remember that it will wear off in a few hours. However, if you want or need to get "unhigh" quickly, a few things might help. It's important to remember that many of these tips and methods are based on anecdotes or animal studies and don't have enough scientific proof to make them fully factual yet.

The best thing to do is to try different things and see what works. When trying to come down from a "high," people will likely react differently to the THC in cannabis and the above methods. Be careful when you smoke or consume marijuana so you don't get too high. Always start with small amounts.

Deciding where to go: **Full Spectrum, Broad Spectrum or CBD Isolate**

When deciding which type of CBD is best for you—CBD isolate, full-spectrum CBD, or broad-spectrum CBD—it's important to know what makes each compound unique and how each might help you. For example, one critical study showed that a CBD-rich whole-plant Hemp extract

(Cannabis Sativa L) was much better than a single-molecule compound like what you'd find in CBD isolate.

THE CHOICE IS up to you; however, each has a different set of cannabinoids and a different set of benefits and possible drawbacks. For example, did you know that the cannabis Sativa plant can have more than 100 phytocannabinoids? THC and CBD are the most well-known of these phytocannabinoids.

WHEN THE HEMP plant is extracted, these three methods determine how much cannabinoids, flavonoids, and terpenes are in the final product. Some people new to CBD might feel "safer" with just CBD isolate; however, it is important to know about the benefits of these other good plant compounds because they are good for the body.

LET'S look at the differences between full-spectrum CBD, broad-spectrum CBD, and CBD isolate so you can put your best foot forward on your path to wellness.

WHAT DOES Full-Spectrum CBD Oil Mean?

When you buy full-spectrum CBD oil, always check to see if a third party has tested it so you can see what cannabinoid profile it has. Some may have more THC, which could show up as positive on a drug test, and even some with less THC could show up as positive if they are taken often and in high doses. If there are no test results for the oil, you should look for a different brand. Testing by a third party ensures that the product follows the rules and is free of harmful heavy metals, herbicides, pesticides, and other chemicals.

WHAT IS BROAD-SPECTRUM CBD?

Full-spectrum CBD oil and broad-spectrum CBD oil are almost the same; however, one big difference is that THC is taken out of broad-spectrum CBD oil during extraction. As a result, broad-spectrum CBD oil still has all the good terpenes, flavonoids, and other cannabinoids like CBC and CBG; however, it has less of the ingredient that causes the most trouble for some people, especially in states where THC use is heavily punished.

WHEN LOOKING for a broad-spectrum CBD oil, you should ensure it has third-party batch test results, so you know what's in it. For some people, broad-spectrum CBD is the best of both worlds. It has the same benefits as a whole-plant CBD extract; however, there are no worries about THC or the "high" that can come with products that contain THC.

WHICH IS BETTER FOR YOU: Full-Spectrum CBD or Broad-Spectrum CBD?

You are the only one who can decide if full-spectrum CBD or broad-spectrum CBD is best for you. Without THC, they are very similar. And the THC may be what makes the difference. Even though government propaganda has given THC a bad name for decades, it does have its benefits. It would fit right into the Entourage Effect, bringing its bene-fits, especially when interacting with other cannabinoids like CBD.

. . .

HOWEVER, if you live in a place with many rules around weed, you're new to CBD use, or you're afraid of the professional or personal consequences of THC use, a broad-spectrum CBD is probably the safest choice. CBD isolate is a step up from CBD with a wide range of effects. Yet, it is still legal under federal law, so you can still enjoy the effects of CBD without putting any part of your life at risk because of certain laws and their effects.

WHAT IS **CBD** ISOLATE?

CBD isolate is just what it sounds like, CBD by itself. However, CBD isolate does not contain flavonoids, terpenes, or other cannabinoids in the hemp plant. So even though this might be what someone wants, they probably won't get the same results as they would with a broad-spectrum or full-spectrum CBD oil. CBD isolate also tends to have a higher concentration; however, that doesn't mean it's better or stronger. Instead, turning CBD isolate into a finished product takes even more steps.

MANY COMPANIES ADD certain compounds to the CBD formula; however, this process takes the final product further from its roots.

WHAT KIND of CBD is best for me?

As a consumer, it's up to you to decide what kind of CBD you want. What you decide depends on how you live, what you believe, where you live, what you do for a living, and so on. For example, some people may not notice a difference between CBD isolate and full-spectrum CBD, and some may choose broad-spectrum CBD over full-spectrum CBD to get more good effects without the 0.3 percent THC.

THERE ARE PROBABLY many things that make you decide what to do, so it's best to learn the facts and then make a choice based on what you know. When you buy any kind of CBD, our most important advice is to make sure it comes from a reputable brand that gives you third-party, ISO-certified lab results so you know exactly what you're putting in your body.

5

CANNABIS FOR PAIN

Key takeaway: Some evidence suggests that cannabis or its compounds may help relieve some types of pain.

Chronic pain affects more people than cancer, heart disease, and diabetes combined. Chronic pain is the most common cause of long-term disability in the United States.

PAIN ISN'T ALWAYS BAD. After all, it tells us about the dangers to our health. However, when pain lasts for a long time, it can affect our quality of life in a big way. With the legalization of cannabis, or "weed," coming up in Canada, many people wonder if it is a good way to treat pain.

MANY CANADIANS KNOW what it's like to have pain that doesn't go away. Nearly 20% of adults live with it every day. The chances of having chronic pain get worse as you get older, and women are more likely to have it than men.

.   .   .

CANNABIS IS USED by a lot of people to treat moderate to severe pain. It can also help with the anxiety and bad moods that come with chronic pain. If you weren't in pain, you might get through your day easily and work on getting better from your injury or pain source. It can also help you feel happier, improving your outlook on life as a whole.

LET'S look at how cannabis could help with your pain and inflammation.

How DOES marijuana help with pain and swelling?
There are many cannabinoids in marijuana that can help with pain and swelling. THC and CBD are the main cannabinoids that do this.

THC WORKS with the CBD2 receptors in your body to fight inflammation in the damaged or injured area. As a result, it slows down the body's natural response to pain, which helps you feel better. CBD also reduces inflammation by stopping the body's inflammatory chemicals from doing their job and sending white blood cells to the damaged cells to help them heal.

STUDIES HAVE SHOWN that the non-psychoactive Cannabidiol compound in cannabis can help ease many kinds of pain, from sciatic nerve pain to pain caused by inflammation.

· · ·

How Cannabis Works to Treat Inflammation

Inflammation is often very painful and sometimes hard to treat. We've all bumped our knees hard on something and seen a swollen bump before a bruise. Inflammation is how your body responds to a wound to protect itself and you. What happens, though, when your body goes too far? Can swelling become a problem? What's more, how has CBD helped people with inflammation problems?

Because of the endocannabinoid system, medical marijuana works to reduce inflammation in some ways:

• Cannabinoids like THC and CBD suppress the immune system by causing apoptosis, which is the natural way for cells to die. In addition, it can cause immune cells like T-lymphocytes and macrophages to die, which is called apoptosis. This reduces the body's natural sources of chronic inflammation.

• THC fights inflammation by lowering the number of immune signaling proteins called cytokines made by cells in the immune system. When cytokines are messed up, white blood cell reproduction and immune responses slow. As a result, inflammation responses in and around the cells also slow down. THC lessens the signs of inflammation and stops the body from attacking itself in the first place.

It's important to know that cannabis's anti-inflammatory effects are caused by several immune responses that affect the ECS. So, on a cellular level, how marijuana helps you depends on your inflammation and where it is in your body.

NEW RESEARCH SHOWS that cannabinoids may reduce inflammation in other, more complicated ways. Clinical studies have shown that CBD has an antioxidant effect on the body and can target free radicals that can cause inflammation. CBD has also been shown to help reduce inflammation in conditions like Alzheimer's disease, Parkinson's disease, and inflammatory bowel diseases. It has also been shown to help with skin problems that cause inflammation, such as psoriasis and atopic dermatitis. In fact, many hand creams are made with CBD to help relieve such skin conditions.

CBD ALSO SEEMS to help reduce inflammation in diabetic rats, according to early research. This is because CBD usually goes after CB2 receptors. Doing this can widen blood vessels, which has helped diabetic neuropathy in rats get better. CBD has also been shown to help these diabetic rats heal wounds more quickly.

RESEARCH ALSO SHOWS that the body's inflammation could cause more than 20% of all human cancers. This is because cancer can be caused by inflammation, and inflammation can be caused by cancer. This is called a "vicious cycle." CBD has the potential to slow the growth of cancer tumors and encourages the body to fight inflammation, which can help the body fight cancer.

.   .   .

WE DON'T KNOW MUCH about how marijuana affects inflammation; however, what we know is promising. We need to do more research to figure out how medical marijuana affects inflammation, how it could be used to treat it, and all of its long-term health effects.

HOW TO USE **cannabis for pain relief**

IF YOU ASK a doctor or nurse what the most complex problem to treat is, they will often say chronic pain. Chronic pain is a complex and multidimensional experience because it's a very unique experience depending on the person. How we feel pain depends on our unique biology, mood, social environment, and what we've done in the past. If you or someone you care about has chronic pain, you already know how hard it is to deal with it.

A NASAL SPRAY called Sativex from GW Pharmaceuticals that contains both 9-delta-tetrahydrocannabinol (THC) and cannabidiol has been shown to help people with MS with pain, tight muscles, and having to go to the bathroom often.

MORE THAN 25 countries outside of the U.S. use this product. However, the evidence that cannabidiol helps with MS symptoms when used alone is mixed. Some early research suggests that using a cannabidiol spray under the tongue may help MS patients with pain and muscle tension but not with muscle spasms, fatigue, bladder control, mobility, or overall health and quality of life.

. . .

CBD IS a good candidate for pain relief because it has shown promise in animal studies, is relatively safe, doesn't make people high, and is hard to abuse. Unfortunately, there aren't enough studies on how CBD works in humans, which is a shame. So far, the FDA has only approved pharmaceutical CBD as an additional treatment for a specific and rare type of epilepsy.

CBD HAS BEEN STUDIED to see if it could help ease the symptoms of some common health problems, such as anxiety and neurological disorders. It may also be good for your heart and help with some pain. Remember that some health benefits come from using CBD and THC together, not just CBD.

CBD IS STILL BEING STUDIED for its effects on certain conditions, and there is still a lot to learn about how it could be used.

STUDIES SHOW that 35 and 51% of adults in the UK have chronic pain. Chronic pain lasts more than 12 weeks, even with treatment or medication. Chronic pain can include, among other things, back pain, arthritis, pain after surgery, fibromyalgia, headaches, and neurological pain. Many studies have looked at CBD to see if it could help reduce the effects of chronic pain.

. . .

CHRONIC PAIN

Chronic pain is pain that lasts for more than three months. Chronic pain can affect your quality of life differently, depending on what's causing it and where it is. For example, osteoarthritis, ulcerative colitis, and endometriosis are all underlying conditions that can cause pain. In addition, migraines and fibromyalgia are both types of pain that can be widespread or localized.

SOME EXAMPLES of long-term pain are:
- joint pain
- muscle aches
- burning pain
- fatigue
- sleep problems
- loss of strength and mobility over time
- changes in mood such as increased anxiety or irritability

CHRONIC PAIN CAN ALSO CAUSE a lot of damage to our minds. In 2016, a study showed that 60.8% of the people who said they had chronic pain also had depression.

MOST OF THE TIME, over-the-counter and prescription drugs are used to treat chronic pain. However, using painkillers for a long time, especially opioid-based painkillers, can cause serious side effects like damage to the liver or kidneys. Because of this, more and more people are looking into CBD to deal with long-term pain.

. . .

How does CBD lessen the pain?

The endocannabinoid system is the body's complex cell-signaling system (ECS). We still don't know a lot about it; however, we do know that it controls things like sleep, mood, appetite, and memory. Endocannabinoids, their receptors, and enzymes make up the ECS. Endocannabinoid receptors come in two main types: CB1 receptors, primarily found in the central nervous system, and CB2 receptors, mostly found in the peripheral nervous system, like in immune cells. Different stimuli send chemical signals to these receptors, which tell our cells to respond to pain and inflammation.

CBD makes the body's cannabinoids, called endocannabinoids, work better. The Neurotherapeutics Journal published a study in 2015 that CBD affects many other receptor systems in our bodies and will affect the ECS when combined with other cannabinoids. For example, CBD can cause the body to make more anandamide, a chemical that helps control pain and makes you feel better. Cannabidiol might also reduce inflammation in the brain and nervous system, which could help people with pain and insomnia.

In 2018, a review was done in Serbia that looked at several studies from the last 50 years that looked at different kinds of pain, like pain from cancer, fibromyalgia, and nerve pain, to see how well CBD works to relieve chronic pain. The researchers concluded that CBD is very good at treating pain and has no harmful side effects. Based on this evidence, CBD oil and other products like CBD gummies or

CBD creams on the skin may help people with chronic pain.

CBD TO TREAT Headaches

Migraines are tough to deal with and are much worse than a regular headaches. Migraine attacks can last up to 72 hours; during that time, even moving or being exposed to light or noise can worsen your symptoms. Many people need strong painkillers to get through these attacks; however, these painkillers often have dangerous side effects. Because of this, more and more people are looking for natural ways to treat their condition, and CBD could be one of them.

EVEN THOUGH THERE hasn't been a lot of research on CBD and migraines yet, we know from other research that CBD can help with some of the symptoms that come with a migraine. For example, you might feel neck pain, soreness, or nausea when you have a migraine. CBD could help relieve these symptoms.

SOME MORE RESEARCH suggests that the combination of CBD and THC can help reduce the pain and length of a migraine attack.

WHAT KIND of CBD is best for headaches?

As was already said, the little research that has been done on migraines and CBD has focused on how THC and CBD work together. Unfortunately, THC was still against the law in the UK at the time of writing. Because of this, we can only recommend CBD oils that don't contain THC. It's essential to ensure that the CBD oil you buy is pure, so ensure you get it from a reliable source.

WE ALSO SUGGEST LOOKING at the amount of oil in milligrams instead of the percentage, which is what many sellers do. The problem with the second one is that anyone can reduce the size of a bottle to increase the amount of CBD in the product as a whole. Since the amount is in milligrams (mg), you know exactly what you're getting and can quickly and effectively change your CBD dosage.

Using **CBD for headaches**

Migraines affect people differently, and different things will set them off for different people. This will also change how you should use CBD to get the most out of it. For some people, it may be best only to use CBD when they have migraine symptoms. For others, it may be best to use CBD to stop migraine triggers like stress or trouble sleeping.

CBD COMES IN DIFFERENT FORMS, and if you have a migraine, you can choose the form that makes you feel the best. Oil is the most common way to use CBD. It would be best if you started by putting about 25 mg under your tongue for the best results. Leave the oil for up to 60 seconds to ensure it is absorbed and can get into your bloodstream quickly. Most people say they feel the effects just 30 to 60 minutes later.

·   ·   ·

CBD TO HELP Back Pain

It is thought that about one-third of adults in the UK have lower back pain every year, making it hard to move around. Research shows that CBD may help relieve back pain by reducing inflammation, fighting the anxiety that comes with long-term or chronic back pain, making it easier to sleep, and making you feel more relaxed overall.

WHAT KIND of CBD is best for back pain?

You can take CBD orally, usually CBD oil, or put it on the affected area for inflammatory pain. This depends on whether the pain and inflammation are all over the body or just in one spot.

HOW TO GET RID of back pain with CBD

If you decide to use CBD oil, you might find it helpful to use a pure CBD oil with no other ingredients during the day and a CBD oil that helps you sleep at night (to find out more, take a look at our guide to the best CBD oils for sleep). If you decide to use a topical CBD or both, you should put the topical on the affected area directly and, if necessary, several times a day.

CAN CBD IMPROVE ARTHRITIS SYMPTOMS?

Arthritis, including rheumatoid arthritis, is an inflammatory disease that usually affects the joints in the hands, wrists, and knees, causing pain, stiffness, and tissue damage. Studies on animals have shown that CBD can help reduce chronic pain by affecting the activity of endocannabinoid receptors, which also reduces inflammation. However, more research needs to be done on humans. The Arthritis Foundation surveyed 2600 people in the US in 2019 and found that 79 percent were using CBD, had used it in the past, or were thinking about using it to help with their arthritis pain.

What kind of CBD is best for arthritis?

As with back pain, you can choose to take CBD orally or put it on your skin with something like Four Five CBD Joint Gel. Since arthritis is usually a local inflammation that doesn't spread to other body parts, a topical may be helpful because it lets you target a specific area.

As arthritis can often make it hard to get a good night's sleep, it can be helpful to take CBD products for sleep in the evening; however, this depends on your specific needs.

How to use CBD for rheumatic pain

When you use a CBD cream or gel for arthritis, you should put it on the affected joints up to 5 times a day, depending on how much you need. Each product will have a different concentration and strength, so the dosage will differ from one product to the next. Some people might not find it easy to use a topical when they are out and about during the day. In that case, taking capsules or gummies during the day and a topical in the morning and evening can be helpful.

IBS (Irritable bowel syndrome) and CBD

CBD is becoming more popular to treat IBS symptoms

like chronic abdominal pain, inflammation, low GI motility, and general discomfort. In addition, new research suggests that CBD may change the gut microbiome in a good way over time.

WHAT KIND of CBD is best for IBS?

Since IBS is an inflammation inside the body, it is always best to take CBD as oils, capsules, or gummies. You only need to ensure that your product has no other ingredients that could make your gut even more sensitive. This could be especially true for gummies that contain artificial sweeteners; however, not for all CBD gummies.

USING CBD for IBS

IBS symptoms vary a lot from person to person, so you might not need to take CBD every day if you only feel pain at certain times or in certain situations. Instead, we suggest taking a lower dose daily and then increasing it if your symptoms worsen.

HOW MUCH CBD should I take to relieve pain?

The studies looked at for this review did not come up with a single dose recommendation. Factors like body weight, individual body chemistry, and the concentration of CBD oil used all play a role in figuring out the dose; however, human studies have safely used anywhere from 20 to 1500 milligrams (mg) per day. As a supplement, though, the government says you shouldn't take more than 70mg a day.

. . .

It would be best to start with a smaller dose and slowly increase it until you reach your goal. For example, clinical studies have shown that people with nerve or joint pain should start with 30 mg daily, and people with severe pain should start with 40 mg daily.

When it comes to pain, how long does it take for CBD to work?

How long it takes for CBD to help with chronic pain depends on how it is taken and how bioavailable it is. Bioavailability is a term for how well the body absorbs a substance. The faster a substance is absorbed and its effects are felt, the higher its bioavailability.

CBD oil is easily absorbed into the bloodstream through the capillaries under the tongue when taken sublingually (under the tongue). On average, you can feel the effects in as little as 15 minutes, and you'll feel most of them in an hour. This kind of CBD works faster than CBD gummies or other edible forms of CBD, which must go through the digestive system before they can be absorbed. This can take about an hour, and you should feel the best results after about two hours. If you use a topical CBD product like a cream, you will feel the effects within 10 minutes. However, it will only work on the area where you put it, and if the pain is deep, it will take longer to work.

Overall, researchers agree that CBD for chronic pain has a lot of potential and can help people deal with their pain without getting them high or making them dependent on drugs, which can happen with other pain treatments.

Should I talk to a doctor about my pain before I try CBD?

CBD is not known to have many side effects; however, some common ones may include tiredness, changes in appetite, and diarrhea. In addition, CBD may interact with some prescription drugs or dietary supplements, so be careful if any of your medicines have a "grapefruit warning" on the label. Grapefruit and CBD can stop enzymes from doing their job in the body. If you are being treated or taking medication, you should always talk to your doctor before changing your diet or supplements.

If you want CBD to help with chronic pain, it's best to research authentic, high-quality brands to ensure you get the best product.

Success Stories of People who used Cannabis for pain

Dr. Jacob Mirman is a Medical Director at Life Medical and an internal medicine doctor. He specializes in Medical Marijuana, Integrative medicine, Homeopathic medicine, and Neuro research protocol/nutritional supplements.

Dr. Jacob Mirman shares stories of some of his patients who have success using cannabis to deal with several types of chronic pain:

. . .

STORY ONE: **Victory over fibromyalgia/chronic pain**

Dr. Jacob Mirman shares the story of a 73 years old woman who has fibromyalgia, neck pain, back pain, headaches, and general chronic pain. She was certified for medicinal cannabis due to these conditions. She is now using cannabis; consequently, she reports being much better able to relax. She is also glad to be feeling a significant decrease in the amount of pain she is experiencing, in addition to a much-improved sense of overall well-being.

STORY TWO: **Victory over fibromyalgia/chronic pain**

Dr. Mirman shares another story of a 53-year-old man suffering from fibromyalgia and persistent pain from several injuries. When he initially saw the patient, he was using an opiate called Oxycodone five times a day and Naproxen, a potentially deadly medicine. These medications did not relieve his discomfort and reduced his testosterone to dangerous levels. By October, he began using medicinal marijuana in August and was entirely off all of his prescription pain meds. His discomfort is now bearable, his testosterone level has returned to normal, and he has had no adverse effects from cannabis. This has been a genuinely life-changing therapy for him. And his success seems to be the rule rather than the exception.

STORY THREE: **Victory over Tourette's syndrome**

A 30-year-old lady with Tourette's syndrome came to see Dr. Mirman for her annual medicinal marijuana re-certification. Her condition was evident at first look. She was tight and had regular twitches and groans as she tried to regulate her thinking to stay courteous. This syndrome produces twitches, jerks, and a strong impulse to swear profanely in public. She is currently on cannabis and doing well. The strain has significantly decreased. During the session, she sat quietly and explained how medicinal cannabis had altered her life. This woman's experience with cannabis for Tourette's disease has been life-changing.

6

CANNABIS FOR DIGESTION

Key takeaway: Despite challenges to and limits of formal research on medical cannabis, many people report symptom relief of certain digestive disorders, such as irritable bowel syndrome and inflammatory bowel disease, which includes Crohn's disease and ulcerative colitis.

https://www.healthgrades.com/right-care/digestive-health/how-cannabis-is-used-to-relieve-digestive-disorders#:

NOT ONLY IS it uncomfortable and painful to have an unhealthy gut, but it can also seriously hurt your health. An unhealthy gut bacteria can lead to depression and anxiety and make you more likely to get diabetes and be overweight, among other health problems. Even though you might think of bacteria as something bad, the good bacterias in your gut are very important to your health. You might be surprised by how much the health of your gut can affect your whole body.

· · ·

RESEARCH at the Johns Hopkins Medical School shows that a big part of your immune system is in your GI tract. Studies show that a healthy gut is essential for immune homeostasis, that your gut can affect your allergies, and that an unhealthy gut may be linked to diseases like depression and cancer.

RUDOLPH BEDFORD, MD, a gastroenterologist at Providence Saint John's Health Center in Santa Monica, CA, says that all of the body's energy comes from the gut. "The gut can tell much about how the body works as a whole."

HOW GUT HEALTH is related to General Health in a Way That Can't Be Broken

Gut health is linked to many parts of overall health, like mood, brain function, immunity, and the digestive system.

PEOPLE STAY healthy because of the bacteria in their bodies, most of which are in the gut. It may seem strange to think that bacteria live in our bodies and that we need them there for good health; however, these bacteria are essential. These organisms help the body break down food and keep the immune system healthy.

THE MICROBIOME of a Person

The "microbiome" is what most people call the collection of bacteria in our bodies. The microbiome comprises microbes that can help and hurt the body. Most of them are helpful; however, a small number are harmful.

A BABY'S microbiome is first affected by its mother and then by what they are exposed to in its environment. Microorganisms are spread to babies when they are born vaginally and again when they are breastfed. The pureed and solid food they eat later, the liquids they drink, and everything else they put in their mouths all affects their unique microbiome.

WHEN THEY ARE in the right amount, good bacterias in the gut are good for the body in many ways. They have even been shown to stop allergies by teaching the immune system how to respond to pathogens and non-harmful antigens in the body correctly. However, even though bacteria are supposed to be good for the body, if there are too many or too few, they can cause many health problems.

IN OTHER WORDS, a microbiome that is in good shape is very good for the body. Also, a healthy body starts with a healthy gut.

THE IMMUNE SYSTEM and The Microbiome

The immune system and the microbiome are very closely linked. The gut is where our immune system starts. If it's working right, it tells our immune system which are friends and which are enemies and gives it the tools needed to fight off foreign invaders. In the end, a robust immune system is supported by a healthy, diverse microbiome. And the other way around, the worse your gut health, the worse your immune system is.

The Second Brain

Even though we don't have two brains, the enteric nervous system (ENS) is sometimes called the "second brain" because it is vital to our health.

The ENS is a network of nerve cells in the GI tract that controls almost every part of digestion, such as the movement of the digestive tract and the production of digestive factors like enzymes. As a result, it can change your mood and how often you need to go to the bathroom.

For a long time, researchers and doctors thought IBS and other bowel problems caused anxiety and depression. However, research suggests that it could also be the other way around. In a nutshell, the research shows that your digestive health may affect your mental health and mood.

More than a Gut Feeling: Cannabis and CBD for Digestive Disorders

In the last few years, there has been more interest in using medical marijuana to treat disorders of the digestive system (GI disorders). Studies have shown that up to 15% of people with GI disorders use medical marijuana to treat their symptoms. Most of these people said marijuana was "beneficial" for their symptoms.

TRADITIONAL TREATMENTS for severe GI problems don't always work well and often have harmful side effects. Some people may find that cannabis helps them feel better when other treatments haven't worked.

WHAT ARE GASTROINTESTINAL DISORDERS?

GI disorders, also known as "tummy problems," are problems with the digestive system. The digestive system is an extensive, complicated system that breaks food into smaller pieces. This lets us get the vitamins, minerals, and nutrients our bodies need while also getting rid of the waste our bodies can't use.

Some digestive problems, like stomach aches, diarrhea, and constipation, aren't too bad and are pretty common. Nevertheless, some GI disorders, like IBS, Crohn's disease, and ulcerative colitis, can be painful and hard to live with (UC). These GI problems can affect a person's quality of life in a big way.

IRRITABLE BOWEL SYNDROME (IBS)

IBS makes the colon hurt (large bowel). Even though it won't kill you, it can make some people uncomfortable. Some of the signs of IBS are:

- pain or discomfort in the stomach
- bloating
- persistent constipation, diarrhea, or a combination of both

· · ·

EVEN THOUGH IT'S unclear what causes IBS, some things can make some people feel sick. Diet, stress, infections, and certain medicines are all common causes.

CROHN'S DISEASE

Crohn's disease is an inflammatory bowel disease (IBD) that causes painful swelling and redness in the GI tract. It can affect the mouth, the stomach, the intestines, and even the anus.

EVEN THOUGH INFLAMMATION is a normal part of our immune system, Crohn's disease is caused by a problem with the immune system that leads to constant inflammation that damages the GI tract walls. Some of the most common signs of Crohn's disease are:

- diarrhea
- pain and cramping in the stomach
- fatigue
- decreased hunger
- losing weight

CROHN'S DISEASE could be caused by genetic, environmental, and infectious factors that mess up the immune system and make the bowel inflamed.

ULCERATIVE COLITIS (UC)

UC is an IBD that causes painful swelling and redness in

the GI tract. It is sometimes just called "colitis." It's different from Crohn's disease because it only affects the large bowel (colon and rectum), and the inflammation only affects the top layers of the lining of the bowel, not the whole thing.

DIFFERENT PEOPLE HAVE symptoms that come and go over time as the inflammation worsens. Some of the signs are:

- BLOOD AND MUCUS in the stool from ulcers in the bowel

  - diarrhea because the inflamed bowel can't absorb as much water

  - fatigue
  - decreases hunger
  - losing weight

LIKE CROHN'S DISEASE, it may be caused by genetic, environmental, and infectious factors that mess up the immune system and cause the bowel to become inflamed.

CURRENT OPTIONS for treating GI disorders

Some conditions, like IBD, don't have treatments that work for everyone, and even those who respond to treatment often stop doing so over time. Even when inflammation is under control, symptoms often still show up. Some patients even have harmful side effects that make them want to stop treatment. Medical cannabis can be a good alternative when first-line treatments haven't worked.

. . .

How Marijuana Affects Us: The Endocannabinoid System

Cannabis, or "marijuana," comes from the Cannabis Sativa plant. It was one of the first plants that people grew. It has been used a lot in the past to treat many different conditions, such as GI disorders. CBD (cannabidiol) and THC are cannabinoids used most often in medical cannabis products (delta-9-tetrahydrocannabinol). Cannabinoids affect the cannabinoid type 1 receptor and the cannabinoid type 2 receptor in our bodies. In the digestive system, there are a lot of these receptors.

Why it's okay to recommend cannabis

The First Amendment says that medical professionals can recommend cannabis as a treatment in any state. In 2004, the U.S. Supreme Court upheld earlier federal court rulings that doctors and their patients have a Constitutional right to discuss treatment options freely. This made it official. Different states have different rules about who can recommend medical cannabis, under what conditions, and how that recommendation is sent to the proper state authorities. Doctors and patients should know the laws and rules in their state.

Under federal law, you can't prescribe cannabis; nevertheless, you can recommend it for therapeutic use without getting in trouble with the law. A lawsuit brought by a group of doctors and patients, led by an AIDS specialist named Dr. Marcus Conant, led to court decisions that protect doctors. The lawsuit was filed because federal officials had threatened to remove the prescribing privileges of any doctor who told a patient to use cannabis for medical purposes. This was right after California voters legalized medical cannabis in 1996.

FDA Approval

At the moment, there are three cannabinoids on the market for medical use. Both dronabinol and nabilone are synthetic forms of tetrahydrocannabinol (THC). The FDA has approved them to treat nausea and vomiting caused by chemotherapy (CINV) after a trial of first-line anti-emetics failed. The FDA also approves both to treat anorexia caused by HIV. Recently, the FDA also approved a product with cannabidiol (CBD) to treat seizures in children with Lennox-Gastaut syndrome or Dravel syndrome.

Nevertheless, there is no FDA-approved reason for it to be used to stop vomiting. This activity looks at how cannabinoid antiemetics work, what side effects they cause, how toxic they are, how much to take, how they work, and how to keep an eye on them. This is important for clinic inter-professional team members who need to ensure these drugs are used correctly.

Cannabis, Sativa, or Indica, and more: what works best for IBS?

Cannabis and its parts have been used for hundreds of years to treat various illnesses and their symptoms. This is also true for diseases of the digestive system and inflammatory conditions.

As the law has become less strict about how it can be used, patients and their doctors have become more interested in how it could be used in a clinical setting. In the same way, more and more studies have been done on animals and people to find out how cannabis and cannabinoid signaling elements affect the natural course of IBD and its complications. Unfortunately, there isn't much clinical evidence that cannabis or related products can treat the inflammation in the GI tract that causes these disorders.

Nevertheless, both studies on animals and people show that these agents significantly affect many IBD symptoms, such as abdominal pain. In this review, we talk about the role of cannabis and cannabinoid signaling in visceral pain perception, what is known about the effectiveness of cannabis and its derivatives for managing pain, related symptoms, and inflammation in IBD, and what needs to be done to use cannabis and its derivatives effectively in a clinical setting.

Cannabis

Almost no two commercial preparations of cannabis are the same, which makes it hard to recommend. Cannabis is a combination of the chemicals tetrahydrocannabinol (THC) and cannabidiol (CBD).

. . .

THERE ARE THC receptors in your gut and your brain. When these receptors are activated, they can make you feel happy. As for CBD, your gut has receptors, nevertheless not your brain.

Cannabis is often used to help with nausea; nevertheless, it can also have the opposite effect and make it hard to keep from throwing up. However, there have been some promising clinical studies that show cannabis helps relieve stomach pain.

AND, just like with prebiotics and probiotics, more research is being done to find out how to use cannabis to get its benefits.

EVEN THOUGH THERE aren't any specific strains of marijuana for pain, research has shown that it can help with some symptoms. It helps relieve pain by reducing swelling and inflammation. Nevertheless, research has shown that it doesn't matter whether you use Sativa or Indica to treat pain. What matters are the cannabinoids and terpenes:

EARLY RESEARCH HAS SHOWN that using certain cannabinoids to relieve stomach pain works very well. These things are:
- Cannabigerol (CBG)
- Cannabichromene (CBC)
- Tetrahydrocannabinol (THC)
- Cannabidiol (CBD)

. . .

HERE'S how each of the cannabinoids mentioned above impacts one's stomach pain-related issues:

•CBG is a cannabinoid that doesn't make people feel high and helps people with inflammatory bowel disease.

•CBC is a type of cannabinoid that doesn't make you high and helps people with autoimmune diseases.

•THC is a psychotropic cannabinoid that helps relieve severe stomach diseases like Crohn's.

•CBD is a cannabinoid that doesn't make you high and is most often used for its amazing medicinal properties. However, some research shows that it may also help with feeling sick.

SATIVA Vs. Indica

Even though Sativa and Indica are two different kinds of marijuana, many people get them mixed up. Sativa strains generally give a stronger, more energized high than Indica strains. Indica, on the other hand, puts people in a deep, relaxed state that affects their whole bodies. Some other significant differences are:

• MOST SATIVA STRAINS have a higher amount of THC, while most Indica strains have a higher amount of CBD.

•Sativa plants are tall and have narrow leaves, while Indica plants are shorter, bushier, and have wider leaves.

Sativa is better to use during the day, while Indica is better at night.

SATIVA VS. INDICA for stomach pain

It all comes down to what you like. Both can help with

stomach pain; nevertheless, the effects may differ for different people. You should choose Indica if you want to lie down or relax while in pain. On the other hand, you should choose Sativa if you want a more energetic high to fight off the pain.

Does THC help with stomach issues?

THC is known for getting people high; nevertheless, many people don't know that it can also be used to treat health problems. It is often used to treat Crohn's disease and other stomach problems. In fact, a short study was performed to reveal whether THC does help with pain, and the results were staggering.

RESEARCHERS LOOKED at 21 people with Crohn's disease. Only 10% of people in the placebo group got rid of their pain completely, while 45% of people in the cannabis group did. Also, 90% of the people in the cannabis group had better symptoms, while only 40% of those in the placebo group did. Some studies have shown that THC does help with terrible stomach problems.

CBD For Constipation Relief: Does Weed Make You Poop?

Cannabidiol, or CBD, is one of the cannabinoids found in cannabis, which can be either hemp or marijuana. This article is about cannabidiol, which comes from hemp. This cannabinoid does not bind to the receptors like your body's natural cannabinoids, which are called endocannabinoids. Instead, researchers think that one of the ways it affects the endocannabinoid system (ECS) is by ensuring that enzymes don't break down endocannabinoids. Since it makes more AEA, this means that the effects of endocannabinoids will last longer.

PUTTING a few drops of CBD oil under your tongue is one way to use it. This helps relieve the symptoms of constipation that aren't too bad, such as spastic constipation, which is caused by irritation and inflammation. Remember that CBD makes more of the endocannabinoid anandamide, which is used to treat pain and irritation.

SO, you'll be able to find the right solution to your problem if you know what caused it. You can't expect CBD oil to help with obstructive constipation because it can only ease the pain. This kind of constipation must be taken care of immediately by a doctor, who may need to remove the stool by hand or do surgery.

IN GENERAL, CBD oil is safe and doesn't have any significant side effects. As you keep reading, we'll discuss the two best CBD oils for constipation. Many people who have used these brands can't stop raving about them.

FINDING the Right CBD Oil for Your Kind of Constipation
There are a lot of CBD oils on the market, and even the average ones are trying to win the award for best CBD oil. Nevertheless, the best brands can back up their claims with tests done by someone else. So the real question is whether

or not you can tell the difference between good and bad CBD oil. On the other hand, we have researched and found the best brands for you. Still, we'd like to discuss which components high-quality CBD oil should have.

CBD TYPE: Choose broad-spectrum CBD and isolate when looking for the best CBD oil for constipation. This is because they don't have THC as full-spectrum CBD does. CBD helps your gut move, making it easier to eliminate waste. THC, on the other hand, makes it harder to get rid of waste. Therefore, it can cause short-term constipation, especially if you take a lot of THC. Still, full-spectrum CBD oil made from hemp from some companies only has a trace amount of THC, which is less than 0.3%, and can't get you high. Also, taking two or three drops when needed can help eliminate constipation.

QUALITY OF PRODUCT: Even if CBD itself is safe, you don't know if the people who make it follow the safety rules when they make it. This can put the product's quality at risk. Since the FDA does not regulate this product, many companies just sell low-quality products without any oversight. Nevertheless, there are some companies whose products have been tested by outside companies to make sure they are safe to eat. Because of this, we want to stress that you should only buy CBD oils that companies have tested outside of the company selling them.

WHY SOME OVER-THE-COUNTER constipation pills don't work

You might be wondering why you should try CBD oil for constipation when you could buy medicine over the counter. That's right, there *are* a lot of over-the-counter pills for almost any health problem, and constipation is no different.

YOU CAN ALWAYS GET a laxative or something that makes stools easier to pass at a drugstore. However, this constipation pill is bad because it makes you have diarrhea and does more harm than good. Even though it may seem like these laxatives are helping, they can sometimes worsen your constipation.

MOST LAXATIVES CAUSE DEHYDRATION, one of the main reasons people have trouble going to the bathroom. When trying to solve a problem, you shouldn't choose a solution that worsens another problem. You should choose a solution that either relieves your symptoms or targets the root of the problem.

HOW THE ENDOCANNABINOID System and the Digestive System Work Together

When taken in the right amount, cannabidiol from hemp has therapeutic effects without making you feel high or changing your mind. This is because CBD doesn't make you feel high like THC does.

THE ENDOCANNABINOID SYSTEM and CBD work together (ECS). ECS is the system that controls many things in the body, like sleep, reproduction, mood, and so on. So even if you don't use cannabis, this system is always at work. The ECS comprises three main parts: the naturally made endocannabinoid, receptors, and enzymes.

2-ARACHIDONOYL GLYCEROL (2-AG) and anandamide are the main endocannabinoids (AEA). They help keep the body running smoothly, so it makes them when needed. CB1 and CB2 receptors are the most important ones. They are all over the body in different places. The receptors work by connecting to the endogenous cannabinoids and sending a signal or response when the ECS does something. So depending on where the receptor is, the effects of the endocannabinoids will be different.

THE CB1 RECEPTORS are in the central nervous system, while the CB2 receptors are in the immune system and the rest of the nervous system. So, let's say that the endocannabinoids attach themselves to CB1 receptors in the brain. It will help control your mood, memory, appetite, and pain. Endocannabinoids bind to the CB2 receptor in the immune system and help fight infections or diseases. Lastly, the enzymes' job is to break down the endocannabinoids after they have done their jobs. The two enzymes that do this are the fatty acid amide hydrolase and the monoacylglycerol acid lipase. The first one breaks down AEA, while the second one does the same for 2-AG.

DOES CBD CAUSE CONSTIPATION?

CBD doesn't cause constipation by itself, and its

antioxidant properties are vital to keeping the bowels moving. Nevertheless, other things are added to CBD products when they are made. Some users have said that some of the ingredients added to CBD oil can cause constipation. If you want CBD oil to help with constipation, try to find out how the ingredient helps with constipation. To avoid diarrhea, you should not take too much CBD oil daily.

CHANGES in how you live can help with constipation

You can get constipated at any time, even if it's just for a short time. Nevertheless, some changes you can make to your life can help you avoid constipation. The first is to try to drink enough water. Always drink a lot of water. This is one way to make sure your body works well. Water speeds up how food is broken down and reduces the chance of digestive problems.

THE SECOND STEP is to eat a lot of fiber. Vegetables, fruits, and other whole-grain foods are foods that are high in fiber. Since our bodies can't break down fibers, they clean the intestines. Also, spend most of the day doing nothing. Try to be active, and if your job requires you to sit still for long periods, try to make up for it by working out often. The key is to keep up with your exercise, whether walking, dancing, jogging, or something else. This will help you get rid of your constipation.

LAST BUT NOT LEAST, don't sit on your stool. In the same way that holding your pee is bad for your liver, so is holding your poop. I know there are times when answering nature's call may feel embarrassing but don't hold it in for too long.

Is CBD a good treatment for constipation?

CBD oil can help with stomach pain, swelling, anxiety, and sleep problems. It can also help control the movement of inflammatory bowel disease because it reduces inflammation. Even though there hasn't been a study that shows a direct link between CBD and constipation, there is evidence that CBD helps with constipation. CBD oil has helped a lot of people who have tried it. Also, unlike drugs, CBD oil does not have any bad side effects. If you use a particular CBD oil that makes you feel bad, it could be because you are allergic to one or more ingredients. Discontinue treatment or consult your doctor before you continue.

WHICH CANNABIS TYPES ARE RECOMMENDED?

Not all strains of marijuana are the same, which is why you need to find the right one for your digestive problems. We have five options for you below. Please remember that no studies have shown these are the best strains for digestive problems. We think they are the best.

Gigabud

People with stomach pain often said that the Gigabud strain was the best. This strain is a hybrid, mostly Indica, and has a very relaxing effect. It makes people feel happy and giggly.

. . .

People say that Gigabud is an excellent strain for relieving pain, and they also say that it makes them hungry. This strain also makes people feel sleepy, so you may start to feel tired pretty quickly. Use this one at night or in the evening.

Blueberry Diesel

Blueberry Diesel differs from some of the other strains we've discussed here because its THC content is 14–23% higher than its CBD content. Even so, it's thought to make people feel calm and happy. Blueberry Diesel is also helpful for people with IBS who feel sick, a common symptom. It can also help ease the anxiety that comes with IBS.

Granddaddy Purple

The Granddaddy Purple strain is another potent strain of cannabis. It can have up to 23 percent THC. People who have never smoked should be careful with this one because its effects are pretty strong.

Granddaddy Purple is best used in the evening or at night because its Indica effects are so strong that they tend to make people sleepy. The initial euphoria usually fades into a deep body melt that can make you feel so relaxed that you can't move if you take too much.

People think that Granddaddy Purple can help with a wide range of health problems. People often use it to relieve pain; nevertheless, it's also a popular choice for those who want to lessen the harmful effects of stress. People say that the

Granddaddy Purple strain is also great for increasing appetite and making people sleepy, which makes it popular with people who have trouble sleeping.

REVIEWERS of the Granddaddy Purple strain say it works well to relieve some of the abdominal pain that people with IBS, Crohn's disease, ulcerative colitis, and diverticulitis often feel.

CANNATONIC

Cannatonic is one of the most well-known medical strains of cannabis. This is because it has a high level of CBD (17%), which is almost three times higher than its THC (6%) level. Because of this, it can be used to treat long-term pain, like the stomach problems that come with IBS. In addition, because Cannatonic has so little THC, you won't have to deal with any of the side effects of the "high" THC gives you.

GROWS Hash

The ratio of indica to sativa in the Hash Plant strain is 80:20, and the amount of THC in it is not very high. The average THC level for this strain is between 13 and 19 percent. Therefore, the Hash Plant strain might be good for calming the body and removing the pain. It is also thought to be a good strain for getting rid of nausea and making you hungry.

. . .

PEOPLE WHO USE this strain say that after a deep feeling of relaxation, they usually feel sleepy. This makes it a better choice for the evening or night.

CANNABIS MISUSED CAN CAUSE DIARRHEA, hyperemesis, and weight loss

It's important to know that the strains of marijuana grown in the wild decades ago were much weaker than those grown in labs today.

THC, the primary psychoactive ingredient in marijuana, can be found in very high amounts in infused products like cannabis vape concentrates, edibles, resins, and brittle-like substances called "shatter" or "crumble." Also, everyone learns about or starts using marijuana in different ways, at different ages, and with different tolerance levels. This means that each person is likely to feel and think about the drug in a very different way.

WE STILL HAVE a long way to go before we fully understand all the good things about marijuana and the bad things that can happen when people use it.

FOR NOW, we must use the information and knowledge that users and the medical community have given us.

HERE ARE some bad things that can happen if you misuse cannabis.

. . .

PROBLEMS WITH BRAIN growth in younger users
There is evidence that smoking or eating marijuana as a teenager or young adult, before the brain is fully developed around age 25, can hurt brain development. For example, one brain imaging study found that teens who smoked pot had changes in the prefrontal cortex, a part of the brain that helps make decisions.

EVEN THOUGH THIS part of the brain naturally gets smaller as you get older, the study showed that the prefrontal cortex was smaller in teens who smoked weed. This could have long-term effects on them as they grow up. One of the scariest things about marijuana is that it changes teens' brains even after becoming adults. Without saying that people shouldn't smoke weed at all, teens and young adults should be strongly encouraged to wait until they are older to start.

MORE likely to get depressed
Research from the Mayo Clinic shows that people who use marijuana are more likely to be diagnosed with depression than those who do not. Even though there isn't clear proof that marijuana directly causes depression, statistics show that the mental health condition and the drug go together more often than might be expected.

PEOPLE WITH DEPRESSION often use marijuana to help them deal with the symptoms. It can help at first. Nevertheless, depression often comes back over time and can get worse than before someone started using marijuana.

MORE LIKELY TO HAVE SOCIAL **anxiety**

Even though marijuana is known to calm and relax people, high levels of the psychoactive substance THC can make someone feel more anxious. People with anxiety disorders are even more likely to feel anxious when they use weed, so they should stay away from it.

ON THE OTHER HAND, people who use marijuana to calm their anxiety often find that after a long time of using it, their anxiety gets worse when they're not using it. This can make the person unhealthy and dangerously dependent on the drug.

THERE IS **a chance of getting mental illnesses like paranoia and schizophrenia**

This doesn't mean that most people who use cannabis will develop schizophrenia or paranoia. However, research shows that people who use high-potency marijuana daily are five times more likely to develop some psychosis.

PEOPLE WITH A HISTORY OF PSYCHOSIS, schizophrenia, or other mental health problems in their families are told to stay away from cannabis because THC may cause chemical changes in the brain that can lead to mental health problems.

. . .

PROBLEMS WITH MEMORY and the way your brain works

The main psychoactive part of weed is THC, which binds to cannabinoid receptors and memory-related brain parts like the hippocampus, amygdala, and cerebral cortex.

BECAUSE OF THIS, people who use marijuana tend to have short-term problems with psychomotor function. Things such as driving that require conscious thought can become more challenging. The drug also has a short-term effect on a person's working memory and decision-making ability. Even though there isn't a lot of research on this, some experts think that marijuana's effects on short-term memory will only get worse with long-term use.

MARIJUANA SMOKING HURTS the lungs

It's almost a given that smoking weed can hurt the lungs, which is one of the things that can go wrong. Even though the cannabis flower and stem are not as dangerous as tobacco, they contain carcinogens that, combined with heat and smoke, can damage the delicate tissue in the lungs' airways.

THE AMERICAN LUNG ASSOCIATION is striving for more research on how marijuana affects the lungs. It also says that smoking marijuana often can cause bronchitis and make people with weak immune systems more likely to get lung infections.

Cannabinoid Hyperemesis Syndrome (CHS)

Even though Cannabinoid Hyperemesis Syndrome (CHS) is still considered rare, it is very real and unpleasant, and the number of people who have it is growing. THC can change the brain's chemistry; nevertheless, it can also change the digestive tract and stomach, especially in people who have eaten or smoke marijuana every day for years.

IT CAN MAKE you feel sick, throw up, lose water, and give you stomach cramps. What's especially bad about CHS is that many people use marijuana to treat the same symptoms that the drug is causing. Unfortunately, this only makes the symptoms worse or makes them last longer.

HEART AND BLOOD **vessel damage**

Researchers have found that people with heart disease who smoke weed are more likely to get chest pains when stressed than those who don't smoke weed. Cannabinoids and weed are known to make the heart beat faster, widen the blood vessels, and make the heart pump harder.

ACCORDING to an article in Harvard Health, this also means that the risk of heart attack for people who are already at risk is several times higher an hour after smoking marijuana than it would typically be.

TESTOSTERONE PRODUCTION SLOWS **down**

Modern strains of cannabis that are especially strong and can have very high levels of THC are known to slow down the body's production of testosterone. Low testosterone levels can cause a lack of energy, weight gain, and a lower sex drive, among other adverse side effects. However, if a healthy person stops using marijuana, their testosterone levels return to normal.

MARIJUANA ADDICTION and Use Disorder

The Centers for Disease Control and Prevention say that about 3 out of 10 people who use cannabis have a marijuana use disorder. This means that they keep using the drug even though it makes them feel bad and/or even though they know it's bad for them. So even though not everyone becomes dependent or addicted to marijuana, the CDC says that about 10% of users are likely to become addicted to it.

NOT ALL EFFECTS of using marijuana are bad

As previously mentioned, it's hard to research marijuana because it's still illegal at the federal level in the United States. In addition, there are hundreds of cannabinoids in the cannabis plant, and scientists are still finding new ones.

THC IS the part of the plant that makes people feel high. Nevertheless, the plant also makes CBD, which doesn't make people feel high. This compound is thought to have the most health benefits.

MANY MEDICAL PEOPLE agree that marijuana is good for your health and has some known benefits. Because of this, many states have made it legal for medical use.

. . .

IT IS KNOWN to help with many kinds of pain, and in 2018, the FDA approved "Cannabidiol" as a treatment for some types of epilepsy.

DURING CHEMOTHERAPY and other types of treatment for cancer, marijuana has helped a lot of people feel better.

7

CANNABIS AND NEUROLOGICAL DISORDERS

K ey takeaway: Cannabis may be included in a treatment program for managing neurological disorders.

ALTHOUGH MEDICAL MARIJUANA may not be ideal for treating every neurological condition, it has proven to be especially effective in managing seizures, multiple sclerosis, and muscular dystrophy.

https://premierneurologycenter.com/blog/medical-marijuana-for-neurological-conditions/

CANNABIS CONTAINS **several neuroprotective compounds**

Cannabinoids may help treat neurodegenerative diseases, traumatic brain injuries, and ischemic strokes. Cannabinoids have been shown to fight free radicals, reduce inflammation, and protect nerve cells. Cannabinoids might even help make new neurons.

. . .

BECAUSE CANNABIS PROTECTS NERVE CELLS, it is mainly used to treat diseases that damage nerve cells. Neurodegenerative diseases happen when neurons lose their ability to work over time. Parkinson's disease is the second most common neurodegenerative disease in adults. Alzheimer's disease is also one of the most common. Even though neurodegenerative diseases in children are less common, they do happen as well.

IN GENERAL, inflammation and the immune response are some of the main things that damage neurons and make them stop working in many neurodegenerative diseases. This is also why many neurodegenerative diseases don't appear until later.

THERE ARE no treatments for neurodegenerative diseases at the moment. At most, drugs can hide the signs of disease and maybe stop it from worsening. Here is where the fact that cannabis protects nerve cells could be helpful in neurology.

THE ENDOCANNABINOID SYSTEM and conditions that cause nerve cells to die

Scientists are learning more and more about the role of the endocannabinoid system in neuroprotection and diseases that damage nerve cells. The endocannabinoid system is a highly complex way for the body to send signals. It is mainly found in the brain. This human mechanism is fascinating because it is a way to send signals that work backward.

. . .

ENDOGENOUS CANNABINOIDS ARE NOT STORED in the same way as neurotransmitters in presynaptic neurons. Instead, they are made on demand when calcium ions "turn on" the process of intracellular synthesis, which is the main thing that does this. This is one possible explanation for why the body's endocannabinoid system acts as a "restoration" or "healing" system.

THIS IS SHOWN by the rise in endocannabinoid levels after a brain injury. A review from 2006 showed that there were very high levels of endogenous cannabinoids after seizures caused by kainic acid, glutamate toxicity, shock-induced stress and trauma, and stress and trauma caused by shock. Based on how the endocannabinoid system reacted to these events, it seems likely that endocannabinoid signaling is one of the main ways the brain makes up for damage after a brain injury.

THESE RESULTS SUGGEST that the endocannabinoid system may be linked to recovery from neurodegeneration. So, cannabis could be a possible medical target.

CANNABIS HAS BEEN SHOWN **to relieve severe symptoms from neurological disorders**

In modern medicine, the use of cannabis for medical purposes has been getting more and more attention over the past few decades. We know that the endocannabinoid system is involved in many neurological disorders. Because of this, we focused on the scientific rationale of medical cannabis in three neurological disorders: amyotrophic lateral sclerosis, Parkinson's disease, and Alzheimer's disease, through pharmacological plausibility, clinical studies, and patient views.

DEPENDING on the methods and results, clinical studies of medical cannabis for these conditions show different results. Some help with motor symptoms, while others help with non-motor symptoms and quality of life. Concerning what patients think, several online surveys were done to find out how people use cannabis to treat the symptoms of neurological disorders, most of the time outside of a medical setting.

THIS HAPHAZARD USE raises many questions, especially regarding risks like using cannabis from the street, taking into account your medical history, and having bad reactions, which shows how important it is to have medical supervision. So far, most scientific evidence shows that cannabis can help treat neurological disorders.

AS LONG AS patients and patient groups want it, clinical studies must be managed immediately to provide more substantial evidence and ensure medical cannabis use is safe.

CANNABIS FOR PARKINSON'S
Symptoms

Parkinson's has a wide range of symptoms that can be different for each individual person. The way the disease worsens over time depends on the person as well. Some people's nervous system function gets worse more quickly than others. There are two main types of symptoms: motor symptoms and non-motor symptoms. Non-motor symptoms include memory loss, short attention span, constipation, early satiety, sleep disorders, anxiety, pain, vision problems, loss of taste or smell, hallucinations, fatigue, psychotic symptoms, and sweating. Motor symptoms include tremors, stiffness, slow movement, dystonia, drooling, dizziness or fainting, stooped posture, movement disorders, facial masking, uncontrollable movements, and unstable posture.

PARKINSON'S DISEASE can be diagnosed if the person moves slowly (bradykinesia) and has stiffness or a tremor.

CBD OIL's benefits for people with Parkinson's

Parkinson's disease is a condition in which the brain is inflamed. CBD is used as an anti-inflammatory compound, which is one of its many uses. It controls how the inflammatory cytokines that cause neuroinflammation in PD work. So, one of the possible benefits of CBD is that it could help reduce inflammation. CBD may also help fight the oxidative stress of PD by acting as an antioxidant. CBD might keep brain cells from getting damaged by oxidation and swelling.

PEOPLE WITH PARKINSON'S disease may not enjoy life as much as they used to. CBD oil for Parkinson's may help with anxiety, depression, pain, and sleeplessness, making life better.

Can **CBD help with Parkinson's?**

CBD hasn't been used long-term in people with Parkinson's disease, and there aren't many studies to use as a guide for treatment. However, CBD was recently tested in a Phase II clinical trial to see if it could help treat Parkinson's disease. Sleep, depression, behavior and emotions, anxiety, and thinking improved after treatment. There were also improvements in the signs of psychosis. About 20% to 40% of people with PD show signs of psychosis. And taking antipsychotics may bring on symptoms like Parkinson's. CBD may help with the pain of PD; nevertheless, research shows that THC is better for this.

CBD OIL CAN BE USED in foods, oils, tinctures, ointments, vape cartridges, and creams to treat Parkinson's symptoms. Patients with Parkinson's disease often have muscle spasms, which can be treated with topical CBD, and oils can relieve symptoms faster. Nevertheless, there isn't enough information about this method of delivery. Tinctures are another way to get CBD quickly, and they also work quickly. Unfortunately, CBD can only be taken through the drug Epidiolex, which is approved by the FDA, even though other CBD oils have shown that they are helpful.

What are **CBD treatment's side effects?**

CBD users may feel low blood pressure, dry mouth, drowsiness, and dizziness. Epidiolex, a CBD isolate, can cause a loss of appetite, diarrhea, increased liver enzymes, fatigue, malaise, sleep problems, weight loss, and rashes. In addition, people with Parkinson's Disease are more likely to have side effects when they take a higher dose of CBD.

CBD Oil for Shaking Hands

When a person with Parkinson's disease (PD) was in a situation that caused a lot of anxiety, a single dose of 300 mg CBD stopped his tremors. This study found that Parkinson's patient who is anxious and has a movement disorder may feel better if they take CBD.

CBD oil can help Dystonia.

Five Parkinson's patients were given oral CBD doses ranging from 100 mg/day to 600 mg/day. All the patients improved as the dose went up; nevertheless, doses above 300 mg/day worsened the resting tremor and hypokinesia.

How much CBD should one take for Parkinson's?

A drug like Epidiolex, which is FDA-approved CBD medicine, should be given at a dose of 2.5 mg/kg/d twice a day, up to a maximum of 10–20 mg/kg/d. This dose may be higher than that used in many clinical trials of CBD. This means that an adult who weighs 130 pounds, which is 59 kg, would need 20 times 59 kg, which is 1180 milligrams of CBD per day. This is much more than what we see in the studies we are doing now on CBD oil and PD.

·   ·   ·

IN CLINICAL TRIALS with CBD oil, people with Parkinson's are given 100–600 mg/day, and more side effects are seen with doses above 300 mg/day. At higher doses of CBD, the oil could cause side effects. More research needs to be done to determine how many milligrams of CBD to use and how much CBD to give daily.

How to Give CBD Oil to Someone with Parkinson's disease

CBD oil sold in stores might come in a 30 ml bottle with a 1 ml dropper. The concentration of CBD in each 30 ml vial will be different, so if you have a 500-milligram bottle, each 1 ml dropper will have 50 milligrams of CBD. On the label, there should be a list of what's inside and how much is in each bottle and dropper.

FOR THE FASTEST way to absorb CBD and feel its effects, squeeze the oil onto the back of the underside of your tongue. The blood vessel right under the tongue will quickly absorb the oil. Most of the CBD goes around the digestive tract, which speeds up the rate at which it is absorbed.

VAPE PENS ARE the fastest way to get the drug into your body. You might feel the effects of a vape pen within minutes. When you vape CBD, you can feel its effects within minutes.

Using CBD Oil to Treat Parkinson's

When you use CBD, pay attention to how much you

take. You should talk to a doctor or nurse if you need medical advice, a diagnosis, or treatment. Read the label on the bottle for instructions on how much to take, or talk to a doctor or nurse for advice. Always start with low doses and increase them slowly, paying close attention to how you feel and figuring out at what dosage your symptoms might improve without worsening. In no time, you may see a long-term improvement in your quality of life.

CBD for Multiple Sclerosis

A small amount of research shows that CBD may help treat multiple sclerosis; nevertheless, more research is needed in this area. Cannabis can reduce pain and inflammation and protect nerve cells. Because of this, cannabinoids like CBD and THC are beneficial in treating autoimmune diseases like Alzheimer's and ulcerative colitis. When you use cannabis strains like pink kush, high in CBD and THC, the active ingredients affect the endocannabinoid system (ECS), an extensive network of neurons and receptors that control many body functions. Therefore, people with different illnesses can get better treatment from the indirect effects of the ECS.

CBD HELPS people with multiple sclerosis in two main ways:
- Increasing the number of cytokines that fight inflammation and stopping the production of cytokines that cause inflammation.
- Using myelin-derived suppressor cells to stop T-cells from being made.

. . .

STUDIES WITH MICE in the lab show that CBD can help stop MS from getting worse so that patients can get better from other treatments. Nevertheless, some of the medicinal and therapeutic effects of cannabis can also help treat MS symptoms. This includes pain, sore muscles, tiredness, spasticity, trouble moving around, restlessness, and trouble sleeping, among other things.

HOW TO USE **CBD to help with MS**

After the 2018 US Farm Bill was signed into law, hemp-based cannabis products became very popular. The fact that medical marijuana is legal also makes people more open to cannabis. Cannabinoids like CBD are available in many different forms, such as oils, tinctures, isolates, concentrates, vape juice-infused foods and drinks, and lotions. It's easy to find CBD products, especially in the US, Canada, and the UK, where many cannabis products are legal. Even though these products can give you the important medical benefits of CBD, there are many things to consider.

THE MOST CRITICAL AREAS ARE:

MODE OF DELIVERY

CBD and other cannabinoids can be taken in four main ways. It can be breathed in, swallowed, put under the tongue, or put on the skin. No one way of giving someone something works for everyone. For example, if you have MS and also have problems with your lungs, vaping or dabbing might not be the best choice. CBD lotions and balms can be put on sore muscles and joints to ease pain and swelling.

Oral tinctures are also suitable for people who want CBD and THC without heat or smoke. Talking to your doctor about the best way to do this is important. This will also depend on the parts of your body that are affected and how bad your condition is.

DOSE AND POTENCY

Active therapeutic compounds are best delivered by inhaling CBD isolates and vape juice. Oral and sublingual use are also powerful. When using CBD for medical purposes, keeping a close eye on the dosage and how things are going is essential. You should check to see if CBD improves your condition like any other drug. Every person with multiple sclerosis has different needs, and there is no standard dose. As a result, you should still talk to your doctor.

SAFETY and good quality CBD

A lot of rules govern the CBD market. CBD products are legal in the US if they have less than 0.3% THC. In the UK, 0.2 percent is the limit. Trustworthy stores meet this requirement; nevertheless, some products have more THC and other ingredients than others. CBD doesn't make you feel high like THC, so you won't get high from it.

NEVERTHELESS, studies on using cannabis to treat MS use THC and CBD. Manufacturers use different ways to get these cannabinoids out of the plant, and the seeds and growing conditions are also different. This means that there will be differences in quality. Using CBD that isn't up to par can hurt your health, so it's vital to find trustworthy retailers who can guarantee safe products.

Using Cannabinoids to Ease Muscular Dystrophy Symptoms

Muscular Dystrophy News Today says there are many ways to treat the different kinds of muscular dystrophy, including medical cannabis, which made a big difference in the life of a patient named Leah Leilani. Leah was given Lyrica to help with the pain of her fibromyalgia; nevertheless, a friend told her that medical cannabis could help her stop the pain at night. "CBN has pain-relieving properties, and it can also help with sleep and calm anxiety," the friend said.

It did work. Leah finally got the relief she had been looking for for a long time after using CBN patches and topical oil. "A dull, annoying ache behind my eyes told me I was about to get a headache. She told Muscular Dystrophy News today, "I put half a patch on my wrist, and in a few minutes, I felt calm." "My heart rate slowed down to 82 beats per minute. Usually, it's between 88 and 90 when I'm at rest. Within 10 minutes, I no longer had a headache."

A 2019 study published in the British Journal of Pharmacology showed that CBD and THC helped mice with Duchenne muscular dystrophy (DMD). In addition, the study says, "We provide new information about how plant cannabinoids interact with TRP channels in skeletal muscle, pointing to a possible opportunity for novel coadjuvant therapies to stop muscle degeneration in DMD patients."

THE SAME WAS true in 2018, as shown by Nature Communications. The study's authors write, "We propose that the endocannabinoid system plays a role in the development of degenerative muscle disease by affecting muscle differentiation, regeneration, and repair. We also suggest that the CB1 receptor may be a potential target for treating muscular dystrophies."

MUSCULAR DYSTROPHY IS one condition that qualifies for a medical cannabis license; nevertheless, other conditions can be just as bad. These conditions include Crohn's disease, post-traumatic stress disorder (PTSD), muscle spasms, and Cachexia. Nevertheless, the fact that some of the painful symptoms of muscular dystrophy can be relieved with medical cannabis gives hope to people with the disease.

CANNABIS CAN REDUCE spasticity and seizures where other drugs have not worked.

Still, little is known about how medical marijuana can help people with cerebral palsy. However, some studies have shown that it has a lot of benefits, such as easing pain, reducing spastic movements, lowering the number of seizures, and more.

CEREBRAL PALSY PAIN Treatment Survey Study

In 2011, the National Institutes of Health put out the

results of a study on how to treat pain in people with cerebral palsy (NIH). A total of 83 adults with cerebral palsy took part in the study. They tried 23 different painkillers, such as medical marijuana.

THE STUDY FOUND THE LEGS, lower back, and hips to be the most painful places. From what the paper says, "Marijuana was rated as the treatment that helped the most; nevertheless, less than 5% of the sample said they had ever used it to relieve pain."

MEDICAL MARIJUANA and Spastic Quadriplegia

Spastic quadriplegia is the most severe form of cerebral palsy. It affects the face, the trunk, and all four limbs. Most kids with spastic quadriplegia can't walk, and their speech is often tough to understand.

THEIR LIMBS CAN BE VERY stiff; nevertheless, their neck muscles may be weak, which makes it hard for them to hold their heads up. As a result, people with spastic quadriplegia often have physical pain and trouble communicating.

EVEN THOUGH MORE RESEARCH IS NEEDED, THE few studies that have been done on the use of medical marijuana to treat spastic quadriplegia symptoms show that it can help in many ways. For example, a 2007 NIH study says that clinical experience and animal studies show that the active parts of marijuana help control partial seizures, which are common in people with spastic quadriplegia.

.   .   .

ANOTHER STUDY that came out in 2014 showed that marijuana could help stop painful muscle spasms. Even though the study was mostly about people with multiple sclerosis and muscle spasms, spasms are one of the most common symptoms of cerebral palsy.

SCIENTISTS FIND it hard to keep doing in-depth research because of rules set by the federal government. Nevertheless, spasms and pain can now be treated with medical marijuana in many states. However, as of 2022, Louisiana is the only state that lets people use it without a referral from a doctor to treat spastic quadriplegia.

A COMBINATION of THC and CBD is recommended unless psychosis is a risk factor

According to a World Health Organization report, approximately 20 million people worldwide suffer from schizophrenia, with more than 69 percent not receiving the necessary care. This could be because some people are unable to take antipsychotic medication, and others do not want them. Antipsychotic medication for schizophrenics may have some positive effects; nevertheless, it is not without adverse side effects. As a result, many people wonder if CBD oil can help with schizophrenia. Some studies on the effectiveness of CBD oil for schizophrenia have been conducted; nevertheless, the majority are small in scale and focus on a small number of people.

Furthermore, they do not provide sufficient scientific evidence to claim that CBD oil may help with schizophrenia confidently. This blog does not recommend CBD oil for curing, healing, or treating schizophrenia; instead, it investigates what existing studies say about CBD oil and the limitations of such studies. Meanwhile, if someone decides to use CBD oil for schizophrenia, they should consult a doctor first.

What Research Says About CBD Oil and Schizophrenia

CBD oil research is limited, in part because the cannabinoid was only recently legalized, and legal issues hampered CBD research for a long time. However, one outstanding study on the effects of CBD oil on schizophrenia was conducted by Kopelli et al. (2020), indicating that CBD oil may help with cognition and psychosis. These studies, however, are limited because they mainly focus on small populations, the results of which cannot be used to support scientific claims and evidence for CBD oil helping with schizophrenia. CBD oil or CBD-infused products are not recommended for the treatment of schizophrenia, according to research.

Can CBD Oil Aid in the Treatment of Psychosis?

Psychosis is the loss of one's sense of reality and is at the heart of schizophrenia in those who suffer from it. Because of psychosis, a schizophrenic person may begin hallucinating, speaking, or acting without thought. Davies and Bhattacharyya (2019) reported that CBD oil reduced some schizophrenia symptoms. The study was limited, however, because it only included 36-88 people, a population too small to support scientific claims. As a result, more scientific studies with more convincing evidence on the effectiveness of CBD oil for schizophrenia are required to know the effectiveness of CBD oil on schizophrenia symptoms.

CELEBRITIES WHO USE cannabis for neuro issues

Policymakers and legislative bodies in many parts of the world still prohibit the expansion and utilization of Marijuana.

LEGALIZING marijuana in many countries will be difficult, especially if the focus remains one-sided decision-making that only sees marijuana as a high-end stimulant with Cannabis chemicals that cause addiction.

LIVING without pain is possibly the best feeling in the world. True life stories have revealed that marijuana use can incredibly save lives by assisting patients in relieving excruciating pain caused by sclerosis and rectal cancer. Some of the stories are written by celebrities regarded as role models and mentors by society.

Tommy Chong

Tommy Chong is one of the world's most celebrities; he is a talented comedian best known for his role in the Grammy Award-winning comedy Cheech & Chong. Chong has been battling Rectal and Prostate Cancer with the help of Hemp oil and Cannabis since 2012 and has successfully defended himself from the defects of the two chronic diseases. Tommy openly declared in an interview with CNN's Don Lemon that he was smoking marijuana as a medicine to treat prostate cancer and went on to advocate for its legalization. He has since continued to promote the use of marijuana to treat illness live on air.

WHOOPI GOLDBERG

Whoopi Goldberg is an accomplished actress who has long advocated using marijuana to treat medical conditions. She has maintained a close relationship with her Vape Pen and has spoken about it on numerous occasions, particularly when advocating for the use of Medical Marijuana. Whoopi's life has improved since she began using marijuana to treat her glaucoma. Taking a sip from the Vape Pen has improved her life by relieving pain, stress, pressure, and discomfort.

Melissa Etheridge

Melissa Etheridge, the famous rock star, was diagnosed with breast cancer in 2004, and for the past 12 years, she has used marijuana to treat gastrointestinal issues caused by her cancer.

Morgan Freeman

Morgan Freeman, 78, was diagnosed with fibromyalgia following a near-fatal car accident that caused nerve damage in his hand. Morgan uses marijuana as a pain reliever to alleviate his chronic pain, which has proven effective.

MONTEL WILLIAMS

Montel Williams attributes his pain relief to Medical Marijuana. Montel Williams was diagnosed with Sclerosis, which caused him severe pain. However, he claims that since he began using marijuana, his life has changed and that he will continue to use it until his death.

Lady Gaga

Lady Gaga is one of the most talented musicians alive today. She has been using marijuana not only for musical inspiration nevertheless also to treat a medical condition. After hip surgery in 2013, the music star told Attitude Magazine that smoking marijuana helped relieve her pain.

Oliver Stone

Oliver Stone has long advocated for the legalization of marijuana, claiming that it saved him from going insane. The well-known actor was severely injured while serving in Vietnam. He confirms that most of his platoon members frequently smoked marijuana to help them relax and maintain a healthy state of mind even when they returned home to their families.

NATE DIAZ

The possibility of trauma and injury is common among NMA and UFC fighters. Nate Diaz, a former UFC champion, admitted to using a Vape Pen to Smoke Marijuana CBD oil to relieve pain, heal injuries, and focus.

Snoop Dog

Snoop Dog is rarely seen without a marijuana joint in his mouth. The famous rapper has been using marijuana for years to help him with his Glaucoma treatment and has consistently supported and advocated for marijuana use and legalization.

MICHAEL J. FOX

Many people familiar with Michael J. Fox know that he has Parkinson's disease. Michael J. Fox has been using marijuana to combat the symptoms of his chronic disease since he was diagnosed. It has allowed him to continue acting and entertaining his fans.

8

———

SOURCE AND SUPPLY

Key takeaway: With so many cannabis products becoming available globally, you must do your homework to ensure you are using good-quality supplements.

"IF A THING'S WORTH DOING, it's worth doing well." ~ Chinese Proverb

KNOWING which Cannabis Products are Quality

Everyone wants to get the most out of what they buy, and the marijuana market is no exception. If you occasionally buy cannabis products, you probably have the same way of thinking. That being said, how do you know if the cannabis you're getting is good? Before you buy something, there must be some way to figure out how good it is. Beginners often miss this because they think that all marijuana products are the same. The truth is that you have to be educated to tell the good cannabis from the bad.

. . .

YOU MIGHT FEEL the urge to go on a shopping spree soon, so knowing how to get what you want is essential. The price and the quality of cannabis products are two important things to consider. Once you have the best things, you're sure to have a good time. Next, we will discuss how to look at the quality of cannabis supplies fundamentally. This will help you know what to look for when you go to a local cannabis dispensary or shop online.

GOOD QUALITY versus bad quality cannabis

Regarding cannabis products, quality is important, especially if you care about how they make you feel and the whole experience. Good weed has a reputation for meeting people's needs in the best way possible. If you can pay for these things, they are the best choice. Bad weed might not be up to par; good buds would make you want more and have many health benefits. This is why intelligent people who go to marijuana dispensaries tend to compare their options. You are the same as them, of course.

WHEN YOU GO SHOPPING for weed products, you likely have a list. Considering how much money you spend to feel good and calm down, that's a good habit. Nevertheless, if you are new to this business, you should learn about the different cannabis products and which stores sell the best ones. However, it's okay not to know everything all at once. You can ask the staff at a cannabis dispensary to help you choose the right product for your needs.

. . .

FOUR WAYS TO **gauge the quality of cannabis**

It's easy to pick any marijuana product randomly without thinking about how good it is. Nevertheless, that's not how it works if you want to be happy. There are a few correct ways to tell if the cannabis you're buying is good. So, if you want to get the most out of every dollar you spend, here are the most important things to keep in mind as you look at the many options:

CHECK **out how the cannabis looks.**

As you look for weed products, it may seem like they are all the same. Nevertheless, if you look more closely, you'll see that there is good cannabis and bad cannabis. There are a few visual clues that show how nice the flowers are. Most of the time, they have a lot of bright colors and are nice to look at. You'll often see them with dark green leaves, fiery red or orange hairs, deep purple to bright blue colors, and fresh and thick buds.

TRICHOMES ARE ALSO FOUND in cannabis flowers. The amount and health of these plant parts are also signs of quality that can be seen. They look like tiny, sparkling crystals on the plant's surface, making and holding the chemicals that give the flower its taste, smell, and effects. The flower is at its strongest if you can see the frosty trichome with your own eyes. You could also use a magnifying glass to get closer to the items as you look at them.

CHECK **To See If Cannabis Smells**

Yes, it's like some food: the better it smells, the better it tastes. If the cannabis has a strong, pleasant smell, the flower is grown and dried to the highest standards. Some types have a strong smell that is usually called "dank" and is a sign of how good the cannabis is. As there are many options, there are also many words to describe how each one smells, like pine, skunk, and diesel. That's because each strain of cannabis is different. Nevertheless, all high-quality cannabis has one thing in common: it smells good and stands out.

CHECK **the shape of the Cannabis flower.**

The shape and make-up of cannabis can also tell you about its quality. For example, if the Sativa-leaning flower is light and fluffy, it means that it was grown and treated by professionals. When it comes to Indicas, on the other hand, quality means that the flower structure is tighter and denser. On the other hand, some growers use plant growth regulators that make brick weeds or rock-hard flowers that might not taste good. Another red flag is that the flowers are very fluffy. This usually means that the cannabis plant did not get enough light and was not grown to its fullest potential. In other words, the shape of the flower is not always a good indicator of how cannabis will make you feel.

CHECK **how cannabis makes you feel.**

How the cannabis flower feels when you touch it is another way to tell how good it is. The best way to tell is if it feels sticky and slightly spongy when you touch or gently squeeze it. When you check the stems, they should break, and the bud should be easy to break apart, but not so dry that it falls apart when you touch it. Mould and mildew can't grow on plant buds that are too soft or wet.

Other qualities of a good cannabis

To find the best cannabis, you might have to research where the products come from and how they are made. So, if you're still not sure about the quality of different kinds of weed after looking more closely at their traits, here are a few more things to think about to make a better choice:

ETHICAL CANNABIS CULTIVATION

When you check the quality of the products at a local dispensary, don't forget to look at how they were grown. It's supposed to be ethical, meaning that organic fertilizers and sustainable farming practices have been used. To do this, you would have to look closely at the people who make cannabis, especially their history and reputation in the industry.

DIFFERENT CANNABINOIDS HAVE **different terpenes**

Diverse cannabinoids and terpene profiles are also a good sign of a good CBD product. This content is about weed's taste, smell, and possible health benefits. You can check this information on the Certificate of Analysis, which a good company should give you. The document contains all the information you need to know about the product.

REPUTABLE PRODUCER **of cannabis**

Shopping at a reputable dispensary can make finding the best cannabis products easier. This ensures that the things you buy are made to the highest standards since the company has a name to keep up. A good company can also help you learn more about the options and guide you through choosing one that's right for you.

THE CANNABIS **dispensary's shelf system**

When you go to a cannabis dispensary in your area, you will see different products on different shelves. There is a reason for this. First, you need to understand how the "Shelf" system works because it will make shopping easier for you. It has something to do with the different grades of marijuana that are kept on three different shelves at a standard dispensary.

MOST OF THE TIME, the best cannabis products are on the top shelf. They were grown, treated to the highest standards, and dried to perfection. You will also find that these things have a lot of THC. On the middle shelf, you can find the average types of marijuana. This grouping is based on their strength, which might be enough for people with a high tolerance for THC. This could be a good choice if you can't afford the best marijuana.

IF YOU LOOK at the products on the bottom shelf, you'll find the cheapest ones with the least potent bud. Some of these products are made by mixing clippings from different strains or pieces of nugs that have broken off and fallen into other jars. This choice is usually suggested for people who are just starting and are still figuring out how much they can handle. Nevertheless, intermediate and heavy cannabis users can also choose these products if they fit their needs and budget.

WHEN YOU SHOP for good cannabis in online stores, things are different. On the website, you can quickly look at several products on several pages. You can also check out the items by reading about them and looking at their pictures. Nevertheless, each store is different, so every online shop you visit will have its features. In addition, you can talk to their customer service if you have questions or want more information.

TIPS TO KEEP in mind when shopping for cannabis
Some buyers keep missing the most crucial part of buying weed products: it's all about quality! Whether you agree with it or not, it is the truth, and you must accept it. All people who use cannabis buy supplies because they want to use it for fun or medical reasons. So, the quality shouldn't be lowered in any way. Here are some valuable tips to help you decide better:

Go to a trusted cannabis store to buy it.
There are so many kinds of cannabis products that buying them for the first time can be overwhelming. Nevertheless, you can make the whole thing easier and ensure you get high-quality weed. This is done by shopping at a cannabis dispensary with a good name that follows the legal and quality standards of the industry. To find out if your store is trustworthy, you should check to see if the state has given it a license, if customers have given it a good

review and if your friends and coworkers have recommended it.

Look at the products before you buy them.

You'll be spending your hard-earned money on weed that smells good, so it's essential to look at it first and figure out what's good and bad. Then, as we've already discussed, paying close attention to the cannabis strain's look, smell, and feel is crucial. Finally, after you look at all these things, you should ask yourself if they meet the standards. If so, you should probably spend your money on it. If not, you can try to find something else at a different store. After all, there are a lot of trustworthy sellers out there, so be patient as you go through the process.

Ask questions to learn more about the products

If you don't understand something about the cannabis product, don't be afraid to ask the budtender. This expert can help you tell the difference between good and bad weed. You should look for someone more reliable if they can't help you. Asking for suggestions is another good way to find the best things for you. Some companies help with product information and other important things. Use their customer service. That's all you have to do. When making a choice, it's always better to ask questions than to guess.

Set Your Expectations accordingly

What do you want to do with the cannabis products when you get them? Are you trying to calm down and get inspired? Are you trying to relieve your chronic pain? There are weed products that are mostly made to meet specific needs, so you might as well look into these options based on what you want. If you have clear goals, you can narrow down your choices. Like other goods, there are different kinds of cannabis products. Look for things that will give you the exact experience you want. Sometimes, all it takes is a little research to ensure that what you expect is what you get.

Quality comes first

Also, the research shows that European consumers care most about the quality of CBD products. Seventy-five percent of them said this was their top concern. The second most important factor is how well the dose is measured. Finally, the third most important factor is the possibility of contaminants.

A TOP CROATIAN company that makes CBD oils and isolates uses cutting-edge extraction and purification methods to meet the highest industry standards for its buyers.

Trust in labels

More than 70% of European CBD users say that quality, dosing accuracy, and the possibility of contaminants are the most important things. However, the legal status of CBD products and the presence of THC in those products are still significant concerns. About half of the people who use CBD said that these worries affect how often they use it, how much they use it, and what brands they buy.

. . .

THE FOOD STANDARD AGENCY in the UK recently said that people shouldn't use more than 70mg of CBD per day, about 28 drops of CBD with a concentration of 5% unless they have a medical reason to do otherwise.

SINCE CONSUMERS' concerns about dosage accuracy are now one of the biggest problems for B2C companies, companies like Ilesol Pharmaceuticals need to give their buyers the most accurate levels of compounds.

EXTENSIVE EXPERIENCE

A reputable Pharmaceuticals makes full-spectrum CBD products and products with no detectable THC on a large scale. They work with several European and UK companies, giving them the best CBD oils and isolates. They have found the key to making customers happy with a lot of experience growing hemp, processing the whole plant, extracting, purifying compounds on an industrial scale, and isolating pure substances.

SUPERCRITICAL CO_2 EXTRACTION is used to make CBD oil formulas. CO_2 acts as a cleaner and kills all microbial bacteria and molds, so the extraction method is known for making pure, clean, and safe products. Supercritical CO_2 extraction is used in the food, beverage, and medical industry because it helps to guarantee that no solvent is left on the products. Because of this, the extract will be cleaner than anything else that can be made by extracting.

. . .

MAKING a new product

Good Pharmaceuticals sells oils made with cold-pressed organic hemp seed oil, refined hemp seed oil, MCT oil, or any other base oil, depending on the client's wants.

WHEN IT COMES to making sure their products are legal, the company guarantees that the total amount of THC in their products is less than 0.2 percent. If a client asks for even less THC, the company will do so. Also, they can sell products with levels of THC and CBN that can't be found.

SOME PHARMACEUTICALS also sell isolated cannabinoids to their clients. These are used as a step in the process of making final products. During the process of purification by chromatography, the company gets isolated. With an eye on how the market will change in the future, the company looks for the best new products for their clients.

RECREATIONAL AND MEDICAL Marijuana

The main difference between medical marijuana and regular marijuana is that medical marijuana can only be bought and used with a doctor's permission for a medical condition.

MEDICAL MARIJUANA

The use of marijuana is against U.S. federal law. Nevertheless, many states let people use it for medical purposes, such as treatment for pain, nausea, and other symptoms. Medical marijuana is a term for products made from the

Cannabis sativa plant used to treat medical conditions and their symptoms. Medical cannabis is another name for medical marijuana.

CANNABIS SATIVA HAS many chemicals that make it work. Delta-9 tetrahydrocannabinol (THC) and cannabidiol are the most well-known (CBD). However, the main thing in marijuana that gets people "high" is THC.

WHEN IS MEDICAL MARIJUANA APPROPRIATE?

Studies show that medical cannabis may be helpful for several health problems. However, laws in each state are different about which conditions can be treated with marijuana. Check the laws in your state if you want to use marijuana for medical purposes.

DEPENDING ON THE STATE, you may be able to get medical marijuana treatment if you meet specific requirements and have a condition that qualifies. In many states the conditions below often qualify for medical marijuana.

- ALZHEIMER'S DISEASE
  - Amyotrophic lateral sclerosis (ALS) (ALS)
  - HIV/AIDS
  - Crohn's disease
  - Epilepsy and seizures
  - Glaucoma
  - Muscle spasms and Multiple Sclerosis
  - Pain that is both severe and long-lasting

•Cancer treatment can cause severe sickness or vomiting.

Is medical marijuana available as a prescription medicine?

The U.S. Food and Drug Administration (FDA) has not approved any medical condition to be treated with cannabis. Cannabidiol (Epidiolex) and dronabinol have been approved by the FDA (Marinol, Syndros).

Cannabidiol is sometimes used to treat severe forms of epilepsy. Dronabinol can treat nausea and vomiting caused by chemotherapy for cancer. It can also treat anorexia in people with AIDS who are losing weight.

What is Recreational Marijuana?

Recreational, also known as "Adult-Use," is when a state lets people over 21 buy cannabis products from licensed dispensaries. This is only allowed in states that have legalized people's buying and using marijuana for fun.

So, which states let people smoke marijuana for fun? Washington and Colorado were the first states to let people use marijuana for fun. More and more states legalize both recreational and medical marijuana use every year.

How are programs for medical and recreational marijuana different from each other?

There is a big difference between programs for medical marijuana and programs for recreational marijuana:

• *MEDICAL MARIJUANA:* People who use medical marijuana must have a state-issued medical marijuana card, which they get after going through a state-run process with a licensed doctor.

• *Cannabis for recreational use*: Recreational marijuana programs let people over 21 who live in or visit the state buy cannabis products from a licensed dispensary. In some states, tourists can also buy products made from cannabis.

WHY DO some states have programs for both medical and adult use of marijuana?

States that have legalized cannabis for recreational use keep their medical programs going so they can meet the needs of their patients. For example, they may extend their operating hours so patients can avoid crowds. Other reasons why each state has its program are:

LOWER SALES TAX: People who buy things for fun pay an excise tax ranging from 10 to 30 percent. Nevertheless, the tax on medical marijuana purchases is much lower than the tax on recreational marijuana purchases. Some states don't even charge sales tax on medical marijuana.

MEDICAL-ONLY DISPENSARIES: Depending on the state, some dispensaries have locations or hours that are only for people with medical needs. This makes it possible to offer more products and hire more people to help medical patients.

DIFFERENCES IN AGE LIMITS: In states where cannabis can be used for recreation, only people over 21 can buy cannabis products. Nevertheless, in some states, qualified patients under the age of 21 can use medical marijuana products for certain conditions with the help of a primary caregiver.

IS MEDICAL MARIJUANA RECREATIONAL?

The goal of using medical marijuana is not to get high, but rather to ease the symptoms of a health condition, such as persistent pain. Even though daily use may be needed, there may be long-term adverse effects on health, and use may seem hard to stop; using medical marijuana according to prescribed protocols would not be considered misuse or addiction. Instead, it would be considered harmless marijuana use. That being said, this doesn't mean this "harmless" marijuana use is always predictable and safe.

RECREATIONAL USE CAN BECOME Problematic

Many false ideas exist about marijuana. Marijuana is not a safe drug, despite what you may have heard.

SOME PEOPLE CAN USE marijuana once in a while without getting addicted; nevertheless, people who use marijuana for fun should know that it can lead to unpredictable and troublesome situations.

. . .

PEOPLE OFTEN THINK that they can use drugs that are addicting without getting hooked on them. This can be especially true when people use drugs just for fun. Nevertheless, it's important to remember that addiction can happen out of the blue. No one wants to think that they will get an addiction to cannabis, and most people are surprised when their drug use turns into an addiction.

WHY DO Marijuana Rules Vary By Country?

Since legalization began, a lot has changed; nevertheless, each country has its things to consider when getting ready to offer new programs. For example, in the United States, when New York said it would legalize marijuana for recreational use, people thought the new law went into effect the same day and went to dispensaries to buy it. However, states can take years to finish the process of legalizing marijuana and letting adults buy it in stores.

BECAUSE OF THE Controlled Substances Act, cannabis is still a Schedule I drug and is not legal everywhere in The United States. That's why the state looks at and approves all marijuana laws, from how dispensaries advertise to what kinds of cannabis products they sell.

WHEN YOU GET your medical marijuana card for the first time, you might have questions about where to start with cannabis. Our team is here to help you find the best dispensary and choose the cannabis products you're most interested in. When you get your medical cannabis card, here are some of the most important things to consider.

. . .

How To Get a Medical Marijuana Card

In states where medical marijuana is legal but recreational marijuana is not, the first step is getting a medical marijuana card. In Florida, for example, you need to be diagnosed by a certified medical doctor with one of several conditions to get a medical marijuana card. Some of the many reasons you can get a medical marijuana card in Florida include:

- Cancer
    - Epilepsy
    - Glaucoma
    - HIV/AIDS
    - Seizures
    - The disease Crohn's
    - PTSD
    - ALS
    - Constant muscle cramps
    - Parkinson's illness
    - Multiple Sclerosis

A doctor may also give patients medical marijuana for health problems that aren't on this list. To get a medical marijuana card as a seasonal resident, a person must live in Florida for at least 31 days annually.

Choosing Your Cannabis Dispensary

. . .

ONCE A DOCTOR HAS TOLD you to use medical marijuana and you've been added to the Medical Marijuana Use Registry, you'll get your medical marijuana card. As soon as that happens, you can go to a dispensary in your area in Florida. Don't worry about going to the dispensary for the first time. The staff will be amiable and open to meeting new people who use cannabis. Find a dispensary near you and plan to go there for the first time.

WHEN YOU GET THERE, let them know this is your first visit. The staff will pay special attention to guiding you through the process and ensuring you're comfortable at every step. You will need to show proof of who you are and your medical marijuana card, so bring them with you. You'll be welcomed into the dispensary and told about all the different products.

WORKING With a Patient Caregiver

Different dispensaries will call their employees by different names. Some call them "budtenders," while others call them "patient caregivers." We call the people who work at Fluent "curators" a lot of the time. No matter what you call these people, you can count on them to help you figure out how to use the menu at a dispensary. They will be able to tell you the basics, answer your questions about different products, and talk to you about the different strains.

KINDS OF MARIJUANA products

There are many different kinds of medical cannabis products on the market. Take your time to learn about what a dispensary offers and find something that sounds good. It takes time to learn about all the different kinds of cannabis products; nevertheless, the staff and menu at the dispensary can help you get started. Most people will find it helpful to start by learning about the different kinds of cannabis flowers.

Indica, Sativa, and Hybrid Strains of Cannabis Flower

Each type of cannabis will have its own unique effects. People used to divide strains into three groups: Indica strains, Sativa strains, and hybrid strains. As we learn more about terpenes and how different types of cannabis have their unique traits, we find that these definitions aren't quite right. Instead, we usually discuss how a strain makes us feel calm, energized or balanced. The same is true for edible products, whose effects depend on the strain of cannabis used to make them. Someone else's experience with a particular strain might differ from yours, so pay attention to how your body reacts as you look for your favorite cannabis strain.

Cannabis Edibles

People who use cannabis like edibles because they are easy and fun to eat. They have a lot of different tastes and textures, making it easier for people to find edibles they like. Another thing that people like about edibles is that you don't have to smoke or vape them. Remember that edibles take a while for your body to process, so don't overeat. Start with a small amount and wait an hour or two before you think about eating more.

. . .

Cannabis Topicals

Topical cannabis products are a good option for people who want to use medical marijuana in a specific area. For example, you might only want to feel the effects of cannabis on your arthritic knee, dry hands, or sore back. In that case, you might want to try a topical product like a lotion with cannabis. Then, you can put it wherever you like.

THC Vapes

People like vaping cannabis because it is easy to do. Cannabinoids are concentrated in cannabis vape oil, so people don't have to use them as much as they would with traditional flowers. Some people use disposable pens because they are the easiest; others like refilling their cartridges.

Tinctures of cannabis

Cannabis tinctures and oils are two of the most versatile forms of cannabis. Some people like to hold cannabis oil under their tongue for about a minute before swallowing it. Some people like to mix cannabis oil with food or drinks to hide the taste of cannabis. We've even heard of people putting tinctures and oils made from cannabis directly on their skin.

THC vs. CBD

There are many types of cannabinoids; nevertheless, THC and CBD are by far the most well-known. THC is linked to what many people call the "high" effect, which is psychoactive. People say THC makes them happy, calm, and sometimes even hungry. CBD does not make people feel high and does not get them high. CBD is best known for reducing inflammation; nevertheless, some consider it a sign of general health.

How Much Marijuana to Use

This depends on the person. Some people are very sensitive to cannabinoids, while others need much more to feel the same effects. We always tell people to start with a small amount, see how they feel, and then change their serving size as they wish.

When you go to your doctor to get your medical cannabis card, he or she will be able to give you some general rules. The staff at your local dispensary will be able to answer some of your questions about how to use cannabis and how much to use at a time. It would be best if you did what felt right to you.

Medical Marijuana FAQ

Every state has laws about how medical marijuana can be used; nevertheless, as of 2022, more than two-thirds of U.S. states and the District of Columbia have made it legal for medical treatments, and more states are considering passing similar bills. However, even though many people use marijuana, the FDA has only approved it to treat Dravet syndrome and Lennox-Gastaut syndrome, two rare and severe forms of epilepsy.

. . .

How Does Medical Marijuana Work?

Medical marijuana may be:

- Smoked
- Vaporized
- Eaten
- Taken as a liquid extract

Cannabinoids are found in the leaves and buds of marijuana. THC is a type of cannabinoid that can change your brain and mood or state of mind. Cannabinoids can be found in different amounts in different kinds of marijuana. Because of this, knowing or controlling how medical marijuana will affect a person can be challenging. The effects of smoking or eating it may also be different.

What Conditions Can It Help?

You can use medical marijuana to:

Help with pain: This includes different kinds of long-term pain, such as nerve damage pain. In addition, this medicine is often used to treat nausea and vomiting caused by cancer treatments like chemotherapy.

Make a person hungry: This helps people who don't eat enough lose weight because of other health problems, like HIV/AIDS and cancer.

· · ·

Some small studies suggest that marijuana could help people with the following:

- Multiple sclerosis
    - Crohn disease
    - Inflammatory bowel disease (IBD)
    - Epilepsy

Glaucoma is linked to high eye pressure, which is reduced when you smoke marijuana. Nevertheless, the effect is short-lived. Therefore, there may be better ways to treat glaucoma with other medicines.

How Do People Get Medical Marijuana?

In states where medical marijuana is legal, you need a written note from your doctor to get the drug. It should say that you need it to treat a medical condition or to lessen the effects of another medicine. Then, your name will be put on a list that lets you buy marijuana from a legal seller.

What Medical Conditions Qualify?

Only people with specific health problems can get medical marijuana. Different states have different conditions that marijuana can treat. Some of the most common ones are:

- Cancer
    - HIV/AIDS

• Seizures and epilepsy

• Glaucoma

• Pain that lasts for years

• Severe sickness

• Loss of a lot of weight and weakness (wasting syndrome)

• Bad muscle cramps

• Multiple sclerosis

How much does it cost to become a medical marijuana patient?

At the moment, insurance companies do not have to cover medical marijuana. So, all patients who take part in the program may have to pay for the following:

Health Care Visit: Most office visits are covered by the patient's health insurance; nevertheless, the patient may still have to pay for some things out of pocket.

Fee for Recognition Card: Adult patients who sign up for the state registry must pay $1 for their medical cannabis card. Remember that the law does not say that stores can't charge more than $1. So the average price for each card could be anywhere from $1 to $10 or more, depending on which store you go to.

Product: It is up to the patient to pay for their medicine. If the patient is on the state registry and has a medical cannabis card, they don't have to pay sales tax when they buy cannabis from a store approved by the state for medical use. The price of cannabis products can change depending on what kind and how much is bought.

ARE there any programs available for patients with limited income?

A medically-endorsed cannabis retail licensee may provide cannabis at no charge, at their discretion. You could ask your retail store if they have any programs for people who don't have much money.

ARE there age restrictions to becoming a medical cannabis patient?

No, a doctor can let any patient of any age use cannabis as long as it is medically appropriate according to the law and the standard of care for the profession.

WHAT IS A DESIGNATED PROVIDER?

A designated provider is either 1) a person who is at least 21 years old and the parent or guardian of a qualifying patient under the age of 18; or 2) a person who has been chosen by the patient to buy, provide, or grow cannabis on the patient's behalf.

THE PATIENT'S health care provider must give each patient and designated provider their medical cannabis authorization form. A designated provider can only help one person at a time.

. . .

How do I obtain a designated provider?

A designated provider can help patients who meet the requirements get into the database, grow cannabis plants, or buy cannabis products. It's up to the patient to find someone willing to be their designated provider.

Please tell your doctor or nurse at your appointment that you have a designated provider. The doctor or nurse will need to sign and give you each a separate authorization. Even if you both live at the same address, you will need to give the designated provider's full name and street address and sign both authorizations.

Patients under 18 must have a named provider who can be their parent or legal guardian. The healthcare provider will sign and give out two original authorizations, and the minor patient's parent or legal guardian will sign both authorizations on behalf of the minor.

How long is my medical cannabis authorization form good for?

Depending on your treatment plan, a medical cannabis authorization may be good for up to a year for an adult patient (age 18 or older) and up to six months for a minor qualifying patient.

What do I do with my medical cannabis authorization form?

You should keep the form in a safe place at home. Please

do not send it to the Department of Health by mail or fax. With a valid medical cannabis authorization, an adult patient can grow up to four cannabis plants at home and register in the Medical Cannabis Authorization Database to get a medical cannabis card and benefits.

WHAT DO I do if I lose my medical cannabis authorization form?

If a patient loses or misplaces their medical cannabis authorization form, they will need to call the health care practitioner who gave them the form to get a new one.

KEEP in mind that copies of authorization are not valid. Patients should ask for another original authorization to be filled out, signed by the person giving it, and printed on the required paper that can't be changed. The practitioner may want you to make an appointment to get a new authorization, or they may give you a new one with the same expiration date as the one you lost.

HOW DO I get a medical cannabis card?

Once the patient gets medical cannabis authorization from their doctor, they can call a nearby medically-approved store (PDF) and make an appointment with a certified consultant who will:

•CHECK to see if the authorization is complete and correct;
•Check the information against the state ID of the patient;

•Take a picture of the patient's face and, if there is one, the designated provider;

•Enter information about the patient and upload a photo to the database for medical cannabis authorization;

•Make the medical marijuana card, print it out, laminate it; and

•Give the patient back the authorization, ID, and medical cannabis card.

How do I renew my medical cannabis card?

A patient's medical cannabis card will have the same expiration date as the patient's medical cannabis authorization. Therefore, to get a new card, the patient must renew their permission by making a new appointment with the doctor who gave them the first one. Your authorization form has a section called "Healthcare Practitioner Information," where you can find the contact information for the practitioner.

Once the patient has new authorization, they can make an appointment with a certified consultant at a nearby medically-approved retail store (PDF) to get a new card.

Where do I find a medical cannabis store?

Patients can use the list of stores approved by doctors to find a store near them. Medically approved stores will have a certified professional consultant to help you sign up and choose the right products.

. . .

NOTE: Patients should call ahead of time to make an appointment with the certified consultant before going to the store.

WHERE CAN I buy medical cannabis?

As of 2022, there is no difference between "medical" and "recreational" cannabis products in Washington law. Nevertheless, products that meet the requirements set by the Department of Health have been tested more thoroughly and may be better for patients. There are three types of DOH-compliant products: those for general use, those with a lot of CBD, and those with a lot of THC. The three special logos on the packaging can be used to tell them apart.

NOTE: Any licensed store can sell DOH-compliant products; nevertheless, DOH-compliant High-THC products can only be sold by medically-approved stores and can only be bought by a qualifying patient or a designated provider who is registered in the database.

WHO SHOULD NOT Use Medical Marijuana?

No one under 18 can get a prescription for medical marijuana from a doctor. Also, the following people should not use medical marijuana:

- Heart disease sufferers
- Pregnant women
- People who have had psychosis in the past

. . .

THERE ARE ALSO other worries about using marijuana, such as:
- Driving too fast or doing other risky things
- Lung irritation
- Getting hooked on or addicted to marijuana

PRESCRIPTION DRUGS BASED on Marijuana Compounds
The US Food and Drug Administration (FDA) has not given marijuana the green light to treat any health problems. Nevertheless, the FDA has approved two prescription drugs that use cannabinoids made in a lab.

DRONABINOL (MARINOL): This drug is used to treat nausea and vomiting caused by chemotherapy and loss of appetite and weight in people with HIV/AIDS.

NABILONE (CESAMET): This medicine helps people who have been sick from chemotherapy and haven't been helped by other treatments.

THE ACTIVE INGREDIENT in these drugs can be controlled, unlike the active ingredient in medical marijuana, so you always know how much you are getting in a dose.

COUNTRIES THAT HAVE LEGALIZED **the medical use of cannabis**
So, where are the best places to do weird things in the

world? Not just anywhere. Don't smoke weed or talk about it if you're in the UAE or Singapore.

There are still countries where cannabis is a big no-no, and getting caught immediately means jail time. However, there are also a lot of countries where marijuana has been legalized, decriminalized, or just accepted by society so much that even if you're breaking the law, you're doing it with people who live there. So here are 29 countries where marijuana is legal or, if it isn't, where it has been decriminalized and is socially accepted.

COUNTRIES THAT HAVE LEGALIZED the medical use of cannabis include Argentina, Australia, Barbados, Brazil, Canada, Chile, Colombia, Costa Rica, Croatia, Cyprus, Czech Republic, Denmark, Ecuador, Finland, Germany, Greece, Ireland, Israel, Italy, Jamaica, Lebanon, Lithuania, Luxembourg, Malawi, Malta, the Netherlands, New Zealand, North Macedonia, Norway, Panama, Peru, Poland, Portugal, Rwanda, Saint Vincent and the Grenadines, San Marino, Sri Lanka, Switzerland, Thailand, the United Kingdom, Uruguay, Vanuatu, Zambia, and Zimbabwe.

COUNTRIES THAT HAVE LEGALIZED the recreational use of cannabis

In the past few years, many countries have legalized cannabis for recreational purposes; nevertheless, access still varies across the continent. Possessing small amounts of cannabis is no longer illegal in more and more countries. This has changed marijuana laws so that criminal penalties are mostly a thing of the past. Nevertheless, Europe's marijuana laws can be confusing. For example, some countries have only made derivatives of the cannabis plant legal, not the plant's flowers or other natural forms. CBD and hemp products are now legal in the European Union. If you are worried about where marijuana is legal, you should check the rules before you travel.

COUNTRIES THAT HAVE LEGALIZED the recreational use of cannabis are Canada, Georgia, Malta, Mexico, South Africa, and Uruguay, plus 19 states, two territories, and the District of Columbia in the United States and the Australian Capital Territory in Australia. Commercial sale of recreational cannabis is legalized nationwide in two countries (Canada and Uruguay) and in all subnational U.S. jurisdictions that have legalized possession except Washington, D.C.

How to buy from a dispensary

It's not as easy to buy weed at a dispensary as food at a grocery store. However, you need to do things before you go to a dispensary, things you need to think about while you're there, and rules you need to follow when you leave. Check out our guide to dispensaries below for expert advice!

Before you go:

Find one close to you! Remember that if medical marijuana is the only kind of marijuana that is legal in your state, you will need to get a medical marijuana card before you can shop at a dispensary. Here, Leafly will tell you if you qualify.

. . .

• YOU MUST HAVE a valid state ID/driver or passport.

• You must be at least 21 years old.

• Bring cash. Many dispensaries are still working out their relationships with credit card companies and won't accept credit cards as payment.

IT'S ALSO a good idea to know what you're looking for before you go shopping: You don't have to be an expert on every cannabis strain or know precisely what to buy at a dispensary; nevertheless, it will help the budtender, who knows a lot about cannabis products if you know what you want to do with your purchase. Start by asking yourself these questions:

• Do I want to have a good time?

• Do I want to calm down?

• Do I want to pay more attention?

• The budtender will tell you what to do next.

As LONG AS you're there:

Dispensaries are NOT self-service: The budtenders will be happy to let you smell a product and talk to you about how different strains of weed make you feel.

DON'T BE afraid to ask many questions: The budtender's job is to learn about the products and try them out so they can help you choose the best ones.

. . .

TELL the budtender about any health problems you have: Based on your medical history, they will be able to steer you toward or away from certain weed strains.

BE PATIENT: Your first trip to a dispensary should be fun, and you should expect to learn a lot about the store's products.

AFTER YOU LEAVE:

Don't light up until you get home: Dispensaries already take a risk when they sell you the best-grown products, so it's best not to use the product as soon as you leave the store. It's just good etiquette!

TRY out your purchases and make notes: Some of the marijuana you bought might be great, and some might be awful. No matter what, write down the products you've tried so you can talk to your budtender about them the next time you go to the dispensary. You can also look at your notes so that you'll remember what you liked or didn't like about it.

HOW YOU STORE your marijuana is crucial if you want it to stay fresh. This is the best value for your money.

LEARN THE CANNABIS LANGUAGE:

There are three types of CBD products:

FULL-SPECTRUM CBD:

Simply put, full-spectrum CBD comes from extracts of the whole hemp plant. This means that all of the phyto-chemicals in hemp plants are taken out and then mixed into an oil. So, when you take full-spectrum CBD, you're not only taking CBD nevertheless also flavonoids, terpenes, and other trace cannabinoids.

COMPARED TO CBD ISOLATE, which is made when the hemp plant is "isolated" from all its other phytochemicals to make a 99 percent pure CBD oil extract, full-spectrum CBD includes the compounds listed above; nevertheless, isolates do not.

WHAT IS **Full-Spectrum CBD Made of?**

When you take full-spectrum CBD, you get more than 100 different cannabinoids because it comes from the whole hemp plant. For the sake of the length of this article (and your time), we'll only talk about a few that are important to how well a CBD product works:

- CANNABIDIOL
    - Tetrahydrocannabinol
    - Cannabigerol
    - Cannabinol

Cannabidiol (CBD)

Cannabidiol, also known as CBD, is most commonly found in the hemp plant. Unlike THC, it won't change how a person thinks, and it's usually used to help the body work better.

Tetrahydrocannabinol (THC)

THC is the second most common cannabinoid in hemp and the most sought-after compound in cannabis, which is related to hemp. The compound in cannabis that changes people's minds is called THC, and that's how the law tells the difference between hemp and cannabis plants. Anything with less than 3% THC is called hemp. Anything with more than that is called cannabis.

Cannabigerol (CBG)

CBG is a cannabinoid, like CBD, that doesn't make you feel high. It is the parent compound of THC and CBD, and it helps make the three main lines of cannabinoids. CBG will be changed into one of these last compounds by enzymes in the cannabis plant.

Cannabinol (CBN)

This small cannabinoid has a small amount of psychoactivity, and its calming effects are currently still being studied. CBN is thought to be the chemical that makes people feel sleepy or relaxed.

Broad-spectrum CBD:

You may have heard a lot about CBD recently; neverthe-less, there are so many kinds that even people who use CBD regularly can get confused. Below, we'll talk about broad-spectrum CBD, its benefits, and how it differs from full-spectrum CBD and CBD isolate. This will help you make an informed decision and find the best products that meet your needs.

WHAT IS BROAD SPECTRUM CBD?

Let's take a step back. CBD, which stands for cannabidiol, is one of more than 100 cannabinoids that can be taken from hemp. Scientists have found that when these plant chemicals work together, they have a better effect on the body than when they work alone. This effect is called the "entourage effect," Until recently, it was only thought to happen with full-spectrum CBD products with very small amounts of THC.

A wide range of CBD is one of the three main types of CBD. The other two are CBD isolate and full spectrum CBD. Broad-spectrum CBD products have all of the cannabinoids found in hemp except for THC, the compound in marijuana that makes you feel "high." This means that people who might have to take a drug test can still get the "entourage effect" benefits without worrying about the slight chance that their CBD products will make them fail a drug test.

Is THC-free CBD the same as broad-spectrum CBD?

It depends. CBD that doesn't have THC can be a broad spectrum. Nevertheless, not all CBD products that don't have THC are. We'll discuss how some brands remove THC and other cannabinoids during extraction. By doing this, these THC-free products are no longer considered to be truly broad spectrum.

.   .   .

CBD ISOLATE:

CBD Isolate is a type of CBD that stands for cannabidiol. It is made so that it only contains CBD. When you buy cannabis products, they will usually have either CBD or THC. CBD Isolate is extracted in a way that leaves nothing else behind. Because of this, it is the purest form of CBD because it has no other cannabinoids, fats, terpenes, or other compounds. People like CBD Isolate because it doesn't get them high.

WHEN USING CBD ISOLATE PRODUCTS, it's important to remember that reputable sellers will ensure no extra ingredients could change how the CBD isolate works. One more thing to remember is that pure isolate shouldn't have any smell or taste. This is especially helpful for people who don't like the taste of full-spectrum oil in edibles.

HOW TO CHECK **quality and potency**

Testing CBD oil is important not only to find out how much Cannabidiol (CBD) is in a product made with hemp or marijuana extract (its potency) but also to ensure that a product is safe for humans to use. So testing isn't just about how potent something is; it's also about how safe and straightforward it is, and detailed test results can help build trust between your company and its customers.

THERE ARE **three reasons to test CBD oil besides its strength.**

What is the difference between CBD made from hemp

and CBD made from marijuana? What does that mean for testing?

TESTING CBD's strength is a complex but essential step in building consumer trust.

WHY IT's important to test CBD oil for more than its strength

Before getting into the details of how to test CBD oil, it's essential to know why samples of CBD oil are tested in the first place. There are three important reasons why a company that makes CBD oil should test its product:

*TESTING MAKES **it easier for people to trust a product:*** People want to know they are buying a clean, well-tested product, especially when it comes to CBD made from industrial hemp. Hemp and products made from hemp are legal and regulated by the federal government. However, the United States Department of Agriculture (USDA) and the New Jersey Hemp Program only require testing for the number of cannabinoids. Even so, the cannabis plant is still the same, whether it has a lot of THC or almost none. Therefore, it is still vulnerable to the same safety and environmental risks.

HAVING a third-party analytical lab test the potency and safety of CBD can go a long way toward proving this. With the confirmation of a trusted, unbiased authority, consumers can rest easy knowing that the product they are buying has what it says on the label and is also free of potentially harmful contaminants like pesticides or residual solvents.

LAB REPORTS GIVE MORE *information than just the potency:* Third-party lab tests can find out more about a sample than just how much CBD and THC it has. There are tests for checking a product's overall terpene profile, homogeneity in marijuana-infused products (MIPs) like edibles, and potentially harmful contaminants like pesticides and mycotoxins. Testing ensures that a company is producing a safe and reliable product.

PREPARE your business for future testing standards. Hemp and products made from hemp are required by law to be tested only for phytocannabinoid content; nevertheless, it is the same plant as its high-THC cousin, which is heavily tested for chemicals and harmful substances. Compliance with regulations is sure to change over time, so it's always best to stay one step ahead. Also, consumers will be even more likely to trust a brand if they know it has been thoroughly tested beyond what is required by law and industry standards.

TESTING **CBD oil made from hemp vs. CBD oil made from marijuana**

CBD oil can come from two places: industrial hemp, which is legal under federal law, and cannabis, which is also known as marijuana. This dramatically affects the testing requirements and the things to think about and worry about for each product type. For example, federal rules about hemp only require testing for the number of cannabinoids, not for the product's safety. On the other hand, more safety tests are done on medical and adult-use marijuana legal in a state.

No MATTER *where the CBD comes from, the following tests should be done on it:*

    Potency: The amount of CBD in the oil is meant by the term "potency." The label or package is often written in milligrams or as a percentage.

SCREENING FOR A CBD oil's complete phytocannabinoids profile is especially important for companies that make CBD from hemp and can't legally have more than 0.3 percent THC in their crop or products. It is also helpful for people looking for products with no THC, even in small amounts, or wanting something with a small number of phytocannabinoids like CBN or CBGA.

HOMOGENEITY: Testing for homogeneity can show how compounds are spread throughout a product. This ensures that doses are accurate and everyone has the same experience. This is especially important for things that can be eaten.

PROFILING TERPENES: Terpenes are naturally occurring chemicals that enhance phytocannabinoids' effects. This is called the "entourage effect." These compounds also make products smell and taste better.

. . .

PESTICIDES: Pesticide testing shows if these chemicals were used to grow hemp and how many are still in the plant. Pesticides can be bad for people's health if used large enough. In New Jersey, it is also against the law to use pesticides when growing cannabis.

HEAVY METALS AND LEFTOVER SOLVENTS: When your product is grown, extracted, and made, it can be exposed to many different things. When present in large amounts, these substances can be bad for people.

MICROBES AND MYCOTOXINS: Your oil should not contain mold, mildew, or other unclean, dangerous, or disease-causing substances. Most states have laws that say these tests must be done, especially when growing cannabis.

TESTING **CBD oil made from hemp**

Even though the 2014 Farm Bill made it legal for the federal government to allow phytocannabinoids to be taken from industrial hemp, there is still no comprehensive way to test CBD extracts from industrial hemp. The USDA has rules about testing hemp-derived CBD; nevertheless, these rules are primarily meant to ensure that hemp CBD products stay below the legal limit of 0.3 percent total THC.

STILL, CBD oil companies need to test their products to the highest possible standards to ensure they are safe and that their customers are happy. Consumers will want nothing more than clarity, certainty, and information they can trust when it comes to regulations. This is especially important when more people, including children, buy the product. This means the product should be looked at more closely before it hits the market.

A THOROUGH THIRD-PARTY lab test can measure how much of the above things are in your product, giving you a detailed report on the quality of the product and proving that it is free of contaminants.

TESTING **CBD oil derived from marijuana**

In states where marijuana is legal, CBD oil made from marijuana is subject to the same testing rules as other cannabis products, even if the product isn't mainly used to get high on THC. Each state has different rules because there are no federal standards for testing cannabis. Because the rules for CBD that comes from marijuana are more closely tied to those for recreational use, they are usually stricter regarding testing.

HOW THE POTENCY **of CBD is tested**

High-Performance Liquid Chromatography, or HPLC for short, is a common way to test the strength of CBD oil. This oil can come from either cannabis or hemp.

HPLC IS a process that uses a lot of high-tech scanning of ultraviolet light. This is usually done with a Diode Array

Detector (DAD) device. With this technology's help, the product's full phytocannabinoid profile will be carefully examined. Results can take a few days, depending on the lab you work with.

THE RESULTS ARE USUALLY RELEASED in digital and printed Certificate of Analysis (CoA), depending on what each state requires. You can have this CoA printed or put a QR Code on the product's label to make the digital CoA easy for patients to find. In many cases, the CoA will be sent to the state, then post the results on its website. In either case, patients will be happy with your brand's openness and willingness to test for safety issues.

CBD OIL MUST BE TESTED, whether it comes from hemp or marijuana.

As a CBD oil maker, when you pay for third-party lab testing, you put money into your legitimacy and trustworthiness. You'll be seen as a responsible leader in the growing cannabis market if you build up your brand's reputation as a trusted manufacturer and ensure patients are safe.

9

CANNABIS USE

Key takeaway: There are many options when it comes to using cannabis. Know your choices and also dosage recommendations.

"THE SHOE that fits one person pinches another; there is no recipe for living that suits all cases." - Carl Jung.

METHODS OF CONSUMPTION

Cannabis is one of the most popular plants on Earth, and millions of people smoke, eat, or vape it daily. Cannabinoids and terpenes in thousands of strains create a wide range of effects, from profound body highs to lucid CBD-induced effects.

EVEN THOUGH PEOPLE who use cannabis feel different effects, they all agree on one thing: it never gets boring. Herb lovers can get creative because there are many different kinds of plants, ways to use them, and accessories.

THE EFFECTS and benefits of each way to use cannabis are a little bit different. Cannabis users who use it for fun can take it in ways that make their high last longer or strengthen the effects. On the other hand, Holistic users usually choose the fastest-acting effects with less of a "stoned" feeling.

INHALING

Cannabinoids are taken into the bloodstream through the alveoli in the lungs when a person smokes cannabis flowers or extracts. The effects happen quickly and are easy to handle.

SMOKING CANNABIS: **Popular Methods**

People who smoke weed have a lot of say over how high they get. Take things one step at a time until you find the right way to do them. When you smoke cannabis, you feel high right away. The high peaks in about 10–30 minutes and can last up to three hours.

• JOINT

The traditional way to smoke marijuana. Usually, dried and cured cannabis flowers are used to roll joints; other kinds of cannabis can also be used. How a joint makes you feel depends on how potent the cannabis is. Weed with less THC will have a mild effect, while weed with more THC will send your mind flying.

• *Blunt*

Blunts look like joints; nevertheless, they don't have traditional paper. People who smoke instead use special blunt wraps or regular cigar wraps. Most of the time, these products contain tobacco; nevertheless, some options don't.

• *Pipe*

You can find acrylic, wood, ceramic, glass, and even silicone pipes. Many have "shotgun holes" or "carb holes" that let users clear each hit completely. If you go to a head shop, you'll find pipes in every size, shape, color, and style you could want.

• *Bong*

Bongs aren't as easy to carry around as pipes; nevertheless, there are smaller versions. These clever gadgets range in size from things you can hold in your hand to huge glass rigs that are taller than some people. Bong hits are cool and clean because the smoke goes through water before entering the lungs.

Vaping

Vaping has become the most popular way to use cannabis in the modern era. This alternative to smoking is a mix of technology and weed. Some models are made to be simple; nevertheless, others have specific temperature ranges and parameters that a smartphone can control.

THERE ARE many different kinds of vaporizers. The most basic ones are metal and need a flame to work. High-tech devices have a built-in heating element, can be set to a specific temperature, and have other settings that a smartphone can control. Nevertheless, the main idea hasn't changed: less heat than smoking. Vaporizers create enough heat to release cannabinoids and volatile terpenes while leaving almost everything else behind.

Dabbing

Putting concentrate on a red-hot nail is what dabbing is. The cannabinoids in these preparations are much higher than in flowers, so the effects are much more robust, and much smaller doses are needed to get the same effects.

Edibles

Eating cannabis is a different experience than when you smoke, vape, or dab it. The digestive tract is a different way for the active phytochemicals to get to the bloodstream and brain. For example, THC has to go through the digestive system and liver after you eat a brownie. Before crossing the barrier between the blood and the brain, THC changes into 11-hydroxy-THC. This THC metabolite gives a high that is much stronger and lasts for hours longer. When you eat cannabis, the effects peak in about two hours and can last up to 12 hours.

Topicals

Cannabinoids are also beneficial when put on the outside of the body. The endocannabinoid system is in our skin, which is our largest organ. Applying cannabis to the skin will help to calm and soften this regulatory system.

Sublingual

Sublingual administration is when you put the right cannabis product under your tongue and hold it there for about a minute or until it dissolves. This lets the molecules move quickly through a thin layer of tissue and into the capillaries of the heart and lungs.

HOW TO DETERMINE dosage and know how much is too much

One of the most important things to know about CBD is how much you should take and what a recommended dose is based on. How much you should take is not a one-size-fits-all approach. It all depends on how our bodies work, and there is no official serving size. This section will give guidelines and suggestions for how much to take. As you might guess, a lot of this has to do with our weight, metabolism, and the way our bodies work. So dive in and see what works best for you to get the most out of your C+L supplements and improve your preparation, performance, and recovery.

LET'S start by clearing up some of the most common myths about CBD. First, CBD does not make you "high." CBD can't be sold legally in the US if it has more than 0.3% THC, which is the compound that makes you feel "high." In simple terms, almost no amount of CBD could cause the psychoactive effects that THC usually causes. To put it another way, there are small amounts of alcohol in toothpaste. Nevertheless, you won't get drunk by swallowing tubes of Colgate. So, it's essential to find the right amount for your needs.

. . .

WHAT DOSAGE of CBD should I take?

To get the most out of your CBD supplements, finding the correct dose for your body is important. Once you've found the right dose, you'll not only get the most out of your supplements and feel great, you'll also save money by not using more than you need to get the desired result.

AS A STARTING POINT, we recommend a daily dose of 0.25 mg CBD times your body weight in pounds. So, a person who weighs 120 pounds should take 30mg of CBD every day (0.25 x 120 = 30), and a person who weighs 200 pounds should take 50mg of CBD every day (0.25 x 200 = 50). Your doses should be split evenly between morning and night. This formula makes it easy to figure out how much you should take.

STILL, there is no "official serving size" or "standard dose," and the amount needed by each person is different. Your body type, weight, metabolism, and product type (tincture, soft gel, or topical) will affect how much you should take. For the best chance of success, you should try different doses and stick with them until you find the right one. It can take two to three weeks to figure out the right dose, and nevertheless, once you see how CBD affects your body, you'll know how much to take and when to take it, so be patient and take your time.

CBD Dosage

Tinctures: Figuring out how much tincture to take can be tricky, so we'll explain it in detail. This will be easy with the information from the formula we showed you above. First, you must remember whether you bought a 500mg or 1000mg strength tincture. Remember that our examples are based on only using tinctures. You will need to make changes if you are also using soft gels, oral spray, or topicals.

• Now, if you bought a 500mg Tincture, the whole bottle would have about 600 drops, and each drop would have about 0.8mg of CBD. If you remember what you just read, we recommend a dose of 0.25mg times your weight in pounds. For example, if you weigh 120 pounds, taking 30mg of CBD every day will yield the best results. Here's our formula: 0.25 x 120 = 30mg. To turn that into drops, we divide 30mg by 0.8mg per drop, which gives us about 35 drops (experiment with between 30-40 drops and see what works best for you). Based on our formula, a person who weighs 200 pounds should take about 60 drops per day (experiment between 60-70 drops per day and see what is optimal).

• Let's do the same thing with our 1000mg tincture bottle, which has about 600 drops of CBD oil. It's important to know that each drop now has about 1.6mg of CBD because this product is twice as strong. So for the same 120-pound person we used above as an example, you would now take about 15 drops per day (try between 15 and 25 drops per day to see what works best). A person who weighs 200 pounds would take 30 drops daily (experiment with 25-35 drops per day and see what works best for your body).

. . .

ORAL SPRAY: Each bottle has 150 sprays and 250mg of CBD. 1.65mg of CBD is in each spray. We recommend using 3–5 sprays after lunch or between lifting weights and doing cardio. Look at our PERFORM Oral Spray.

SOFT GELS: Each soft gel has 25mg of CBD, and each bottle has 30 soft gels. One of the best things about this product is that the soft gel sets the dose. For example, C+L softness contains 25mg of CBD, which is one of the best things. When using CBD products, remember that our recommended dose is 0.25mg of CBD per pound of body weight.

TOPICAL LOTIONS OR PATCH: These products, like Muscle Rub and Patch, are put on the skin and give you relief right where you need it most. Just put a lot on the affected areas. You can use transdermal patches or cut them with scissors to get the correct dose. Since they are absorbed through the skin, topical products tend to work slower than supplements you eat. However, they are easy to use and make you feel great.

EASY CANNABIS RECIPES

If you've ever tried cooking more than just a night out or a cup of instant noodles, you know the joy and satisfaction it brings.

WE'RE NOT JUST TALKING brownies either (nevertheless, hey, they might make an appearance anyway). Let's try some of the best food your taste buds have ever had.

. . .

Cannaneverthelesster

This one is a great place to start because it can be used to make almost anything. But, unless you're a vegan, you might not know that nevertheless is in more foods than you think.

Here's what you need to do:

• Melt the nevertheless in a pot (add a little water to keep it from burning)

• Add your ground, decarboxylated marijuana, and let it cook for two to three hours.

• Put the strained nevertheless in a jar (for example, you can use a funnel with cheesecloth to catch the ground-up weed)

• Put the jar of cannaneverthelesster in the fridge!

• You now have a great ingredient that can be used in many tasty dishes.

Bacon Weed

In recent years, the bacon craze may have died down a bit, but it's unlikely that this salty snack will ever be entirely out of style.

• To make your weed bacon, sprinkle ground, decarboxylated flower on one side of each slice of bacon. Bake at 275 degrees Fahrenheit and flip after about 10 minutes.

• Sprinkle the other side, and do it again 10 minutes later.

. . .

FUN FACT: You can now use the leftover cannabis-infused bacon grease in other dishes.

Cannaoil

Cannaoil can also be used as a base for many different recipes. Here's how to put that together:

- Mix 1 ounce of ground, decarboxylated bud with 2 cups of oil (coconut, vegetable, etc.)
- Heat for at least six hours without bringing it to a boil.
- Use water to keep from getting burned.
- The oil from the ground-up bud must be strained.
- This oil with weed might be the best ingredient for a salad dressing made with oil.

Bud Brownies

You knew it would come to this point. There's a reason why it's a classic.

- NOW THAT YOU know how to use cannaoil let's make some bud brownies. Mix your favorite brownie with eggs, water, and cannabis oil.
- Line it up on a cookie sheet and bake it for about 30 minutes at 330 degrees Fahrenheit.

Marijuana Ice Cream

Sometimes baked goods aren't enough, and you need something cold and refreshing. It's surprisingly easy to make weed ice cream, and you can dress it up however you want. Do the following to make it:

·   ·   ·

•About 16 ounces of heavy cream should be melted in a saucepan at about medium heat.

•Melt your cannaneverthelesster and mix in the sugar.

•Add whatever you want to the mixture (fruit, nuts, chocolate chips, etc.)

•Freeze overnight

•If you make enough, you might be able to enjoy a sweet frozen treat for more than one night.

Té de Cannabis

There's no better way to start the day than with a warm cup of cannabis tea. This one is easy, so you shouldn't have trouble getting it going.

Brew your favorite tea, add about a teaspoon of your cannaneverthelesster, and sweeten it with milk, honey, sugar, or a combination of the three.

Weed Milk

•In a saucepan, heat your milk over medium to low heat. Add the ground and decarboxylated weed and heat for about 45 minutes.

•Take the mixture off the heat and let it sit for about ten minutes. Again, the milk from the ground-up weed should be strained (again, you can use something like a strainer or a sieve with a cheesecloth).

•If you put your weed milk in the fridge, you now have a great way to eat weed that you can add to your breakfast cereal.

10

A BALANCED VIEW

 ey takeaway: We need to explore some of the myths so we can better educate ourselves and others.

"EDUCATION IS the movement from darkness to light." - Allan Bloom

DISPELLING the harmful myths around cannabis

The cannabis market has grown a lot over the past few years. People in the U.S. have only heard for decades that marijuana is dangerous. Now, they are learning that it can be used to treat minor pains and illnesses. Not to mention people with long-term illnesses who use it to ease their symptoms and improve their lives. And, of course, some people like to use cannabis for fun.

. . .

EVEN THOUGH CANNABIS is becoming more accepted, there is still a lot we don't know about it and a lot of research. Washington state just opened its first cannabis research lab, and research funded by the federal government seems to be picking up speed. Nevertheless, there are a few myths about cannabis that won't go away.

LET'S clear up a few of these myths that have been around for a long time.

*CANNABIS CAN LEAD **to doing other, more dangerous drugs.***
In middle school health class, you probably learned that cannabis, also called marijuana, weed, pot, dope, etc., is a "gateway drug" that can lead to the use of harder, more dangerous drugs like cocaine, methamphetamine, and even heroin.

NEVERTHELESS, there isn't much evidence to back up this theory. Studies have shown that people who use cannabis are more likely to try harder drugs. However, the results of these studies can be misleading because they often only count one-time users and don't look at why people use harder drugs. There are likely a wide range of other factors, not including marijuana use, that influence their choice to try other drugs. In a 1999 report, the Institute of Medicine said that cannabis "does not appear to be a gateway drug in the sense that it is the cause or even the most significant predictor of serious drug abuse; that is, care must be taken not to bring negative cause to an association." The report goes on to say, "The most consistent predictors of serious drug use seem to be the intensity of marijuana use and co-occurring psychiatric disorders or a family history of psychopathology (including alcoholism)." Also, the National Institute on Drug Abuse (NIDA) says on their website that most people who use marijuana don't go on to use "harder" drugs. Studies have shown that cannabis can be used instead of drugs like methadone or buprenorphine to treat opioid addiction.

So, it's never a good idea for teens to use cannabis for fun; it's unlikely that a few puffs here and there will lead to opioid addiction. Nevertheless, while we're talking about drugs...

*YOU CAN'T GET **hooked (addicted) on cannabis.***

Let's be clear: cannabis can make you get used to it and could make you addicted, but not as much as your morning coffee. The author of "The Science of Marijuana," Leslie L. Iverson, looked at many international studies on cannabis and found that only 9 percent of people who use it will become seriously addicted. However, between 10 and 30% of people who use it will depend on it in one way or another. In contrast, about 23% of people who use heroin will become seriously addicted to opioids, and an overdose of heroin can kill you.

Is it ever good to get hooked on something or depend on it? Actually, no. Nevertheless, using too much cannabis is much less dangerous than using too much of many other drugs that people do every day.

. . .

TOO MUCH CANNABIS can kill you.

As far as we know, no one has ever died from too much cannabis. It's not impossible to die from too much cannabis. Nevertheless, it's almost impossible. The author of "Weed: The User's Guide," David Schmader, says that you would have to eat 1,500 pounds of cannabis in fifteen minutes to die from an overdose.

NEVERTHELESS, you can still get harmful side effects, like anxiety, paranoia, nausea, and vomiting, if you have too much. The best way to avoid this is to know how much to take and to be patient when it comes to edibles, which can take up to an hour to start working and are often stronger than smoking or vaping cannabis.

CANNABIS KILLS cells in the brain.

The myth that cannabis will kill brain cells or lower your IQ has been around for a long time. It's a favorite scare tactic for people who don't like cannabis. Nevertheless, there isn't much evidence that marijuana is bad for the brain. In 2016, the Federal Drug Association said that cannabis has no long-term effects on how well the brain works.

THEY WROTE, "The effects of long-term marijuana use don't seem to last more than one to three months after stopping... After three months of not using drugs, any differences between scores before and after heavy marijuana use in IQ, immediate memory, delayed memory, and speed of processing information were no longer clear."

IN REALITY, the brain, nervous system, and immune system all use cannabinoids, and the body has an endocannabinoid system that controls how they work. Cannabinoids from the plant interact with these to make different effects. This is why cannabis is a useful medicine and deserves more research.

CANNABIS MAKES YOU LAZY.

In July 2001, Afroman came out with the hit song "Because I got high." It was a funny song about how using marijuana was hurting his life. It sold more than 1.5 million copies and was nominated for a Grammy. But unfortunately, it also made people think that all stoners are lazy and don't do anything.

THERE ARE chemotypes and products of cannabis that make people sleepier than usual, nevertheless, there are just as many that wake people up and fight fatigue. In addition, studies have shown that cannabinoids like THCV have energizing effects, so people often use products to get more work done or energy before working out.

AFROMAN HAS LEARNED from his mistakes, which is a good thing. In 2014, he released a new, happier version of the song, which talks about how cannabis helps him with his glaucoma and anxiety.

. . .

"I USED TO SMOKE; nevertheless, after I got high, I quit."

I was about to give up because I was tired; nevertheless, I got high.

I know why I'm playing basketball and running now.

Because I was high because I was high because I was high."

THERE IS STILL a lot to learn about cannabis; nevertheless, clearing up some wrong information is an essential first step to understanding how cannabis affects us as individuals and as a society.

GATEWAY DRUGS, trauma, addiction, and more

The idea that pot is a gateway drug is still debated. Nevertheless, not all research backs up this idea. Even studies that say people who use cannabis are more likely to use other drugs rarely show that cannabis directly causes people to use other drugs.

WHY SOME PEOPLE Try Other Drugs

The National Institute on Drug Abuse (NIDA) has three ideas about why some people who use marijuana use other drugs while others don't. Here's a closer look at some of their ideas:

WHEN PEOPLE START USING marijuana when their brains are still young and developing, which can be as late as their early 20s, it can change how their brains respond to rewards. In turn, this could make people want to try other drugs.

PEOPLE WHO USE cannabis are more likely to hang out with people who use and sell other drugs, which makes them more likely to want to try them.

CANNABIS IS EASIER to get than other drugs, so young people who are more likely to use drugs may try it first. The same is true for alcohol and cigarettes.

THE GATEWAY DRUG Theory

THE GATEWAY DRUG theory says that so-called "soft" drugs, like marijuana, make people feel "high" in a way that seems safe, which makes them more likely to try harder drugs.

MOST PEOPLE with serious drug problems like cocaine, meth, and heroin try marijuana first. Nevertheless, it's also important to keep in mind that most people who use marijuana won't go on to use harder drugs.

NONETHELESS, the argument is that if these hard drug users hadn't started with marijuana, they wouldn't have gotten a false sense of security from drug use and wouldn't have moved on to other, more dangerous drugs.

·   ·   ·

MARIJUANA IS DESIGNATED **as the 'gateway drug.'**

Marijuana has been considered the most common first drug for a long time. A movie called "Reefer Madness" came out in 1936. It was a movie that tried to scare worried parents away from marijuana. The movie pushed the idea that teens who use marijuana have sex and break the law.

SOON AFTER, the Marijuana Tax Act of 1937 made it against the law to use or own marijuana. Then, in the 1980s, marijuana was in the news again because of the "gateway drug" theory.

THE NUMBER of teens and young adults who use marijuana is going up. Most people try drugs for the first time between 16 and 17 years old. One study found that teens try marijuana on average at a younger age than they did with tobacco and alcohol. Even though marijuana is legal in many places, it is still the most commonly used illegal drug in the United States.

IS MARIJUANA A "GATEWAY" **drug?**

The politics of cannabis research and policy are still very heated. People who want cannabis to be illegal say it is hazardous and leads to addiction. So they want to ban cannabis and punish people who have it.

ON THE OTHER HAND, **people who support cannabis say that** it is safe and maybe even helpful, that banning it leads to more people being locked up, and that the war on drugs has failed.

THE AMERICAN CIVIL LIBERTIES UNION says that the war on drugs and cannabis leads to a lot of police stops and a lot of people being locked up. Cannabis possession is the reason for half of all drug arrests, and most arrests are for people using the drug for their use, not to sell it.

DOES USING **marijuana make people use other drugs?**
Even though there has been a lot of research into the link between cannabis use and other drug use, this question has only been partially answered. Studies show that some people are more likely to become heavy cannabis users because their genes make them more likely to use drugs. Nevertheless, this finding doesn't back up the idea that being around cannabis makes people more likely to try other drugs.

THE SOCIAL PARTS of the gateway drug theory are supported by evidence that cannabis users hang out with other drug users in places where they are more likely to try other illegal drugs at a younger age. This creates a subculture of illegal drug users open to trying other illegal drugs.

THE GATEWAY THEORY **Cannot Be Proved**
It is impossible to know how common drug use is, and studies of drug use are often wrong, so there is no way to know if marijuana use and other drugs are always linked.

Many people who use marijuana don't move on to other drugs.

EVEN IF IT were proven that people who used marijuana were much more likely to use other drugs, there is no way to know if this was because marijuana is a gateway drug, if there were other factors at play, or if the people just used whatever drugs they could find.

EDUCATE AND COMMUNICATE on Cannabis Usage

As the movement to legalize cannabis continues, more and more people are bringing this amazing plant into their lives. We are moving in a brave new direction as the negative stereotypes about cannabis disappear. So much new research and information about this plant is coming out, and it's starting to feel like the more we learn, the less we know.

EVEN THOUGH THIS might be true, it's more important than ever to learn about cannabis. Cannabis education is important because people need to know about cannabis, how it affects their bodies, and how the industry around it works. Cannabis has real healing power, and learning more about the plant, its chemicals, and its products will help you figure out how to use it in your life.

CANNABIS IS a plant with many parts. It makes a lot of different chemicals called cannabinoids, which all have effects on the human body. It's important to learn about these different cannabinoids and how they affect your endo-cannabinoid system if you want to use cannabis as part of your daily life. THC and CBD are the two most well-known cannabinoids.

However, we now know that the cannabis plant can make about 140 other cannabinoid compounds. If you learn about these cannabinoids, you'll be able to use them to treat certain illnesses or make changes in your body. Cannabinoids can work together to make a broad spectrum or work on their own as isolates, which we discuss in full-spectrum vs. isolate extract.

You can learn more about what works best for your body by trying out different products with a wide range of cannabinoids or just one type of cannabinoid. The floodgates for cannabis are open, so in the coming years, we will see more and more products made from cannabis. If you know about cannabinoids, you'll be able to find your way around these new products and choose the ones that are best for you.

Now that there are a lot of different product lines that give people choices about what cannabinoids they want to use, there are also many different ways to use them. Every day, new products come out on the market with new and creative ways to deliver them. Even though these innovations are a huge step forward, there are many options, and each delivery method might not be the best for the customer's desired effect.

. . .

FOR EXAMPLE, if you want to treat psoriasis, a lotion with the herb will work much better than a spray or tincture. It's important to learn about these delivery methods and determine which is best for you and the problems you're trying to fix. You might not get the desired effects if you use the wrong method to take your cannabis products.

CANNABIS IS BECOMING **legal in more places.**

More than 22 U.S. states have legalized marijuana for either medical or recreational use or both. Canada made it legal for both medical and recreational use of marijuana. There are a lot more countries following. When people abuse a product that can make them crazy, they need to be taught how to use it properly to get the benefits.

A LONG TIME AGO, when cannabis was illegal almost everywhere in the world, smoking it or even taking it for medical reasons was looked down upon. But as more places legalize weed, the stigma is starting to fade. Now that weed is legal in specific areas, researchers can do a lot of work to find more benefits and new ways to use it for medical purposes. Again, this opens the door to new products that people need to learn about.

YOUNG PEOPLE ARE USING **cannabis more and more.**

Cannabis is the most widely used drug that is against the law. However, at least 7.8% of Americans use cannabis for fun or to treat health problems. Most people who use marijuana are in college. A National Institute on Drug Abuse survey found that young people not in college are more likely to use cannabis than those of the same age.

AT LEAST 13% of young people who aren't in college use marijuana, but only 4.9% of young people who are in college do. Note that people between the ages of 19 and 22 who use marijuana often for fun lose some of their physical and mental abilities.

EVEN THOUGH CANNABIS has a lot of health benefits, college students shouldn't use it. When marijuana is used for medical reasons, a prescription is given by a doctor, and the amount of THC in medical marijuana is low. But cannabis can lead to psychosis if it is used for fun. Because of this, every neighborhood needs to have at least one place where people can learn about cannabis.

THERE ARE STILL **a lot of wrong ideas about how safe weed is.**

What do online resources about cannabis say? Is pot safe to use or not? Some sources say that pot is safe and sound for you. On the other hand, some people will tell you not to use weed, even if you need it for medical reasons. This is because there are many chemicals in weed, each having a different effect on the body.

WITH CANNABIS EDUCATION, you can learn about the different cannabinoids in cannabis and how they affect your endocannabinoid system. This can be done online or in person. Even though THC and CBD are the most common cannabinoids, cannabis contains about 120 other cannabinoids. These chemicals can work together in a wide range, or they can work on their own. Some cannabinoids, like THC, make you feel "high," and long-term use can lead to psychosis or other mental health problems. Compounds like CBD and CBN, on the other hand, are safer and will help ease pain and other symptoms of illness.

LEARNING about cannabis

Even though many people who use cannabis do it for fun, some people need it because it can help them feel better. To use pot as medicine, you need to know the different compounds related to your condition and which strains can give you these compounds. There are a lot of different chemicals in marijuana, just like there are a lot of different compounds in each strain.

SINCE CANNABIS IS legal in some states and countries, many different products have been made, some of which claim to cure certain illnesses. Most of these items have been on sale for less than two years. New things are coming out. Even though the labels say CBD, some of these products may not have any CBD. Other things have poisonous things in them, like heavy metals and solvents. A cannabis education center needs to be in the neighborhood so people can learn how these products work and determine the best ones.

YOU CAN HAVE a career in pot if you learn enough about it.

Would you like to know a lot about pot? You can do a lot of pot is legal where you live. To start, you can learn more about weed and what it can do for you. For example, people say that marijuana helps cancer patients deal with the side effects of chemotherapy. It helps with nausea, loss of appetite, and many other things. Scientists can find out more about these claims. You can also make educational materials about cannabis, develop new products, become a pot doctor, and do many other things.

As more people start to use medical cannabis, it will be important to learn about it. Cannabis education, either online or in person, might help ensure there are no contradictory facts. In addition, as the world moves toward legalizing marijuana, more information is needed about how it is used, what good things it can do, and what bad things it can do.

AFTERWORD

"Some of my finest hours have been spent on my back veranda, smoking hemp and observing as far as my eye can see." — *Thomas Jefferson.*

Now we have come to the end of this exciting journey; however, to refresh your minds, here are some things we discussed;

Since ancient times, people have known that the cannabis plant can be used as medicine. Cannabis was used to treat many health problems as early as 2800 BC. It was even on Emperor Shen Nung's list of medicines.

Cannabis has a long and fascinating past. Cannabis use began in either central Asia or western China. Cannabis has been used for thousands of years because people think it can heal them. It was first used in 2800 BC when it was included in the pharmacopeia of Emperor Shen Nung, known as the "father of Chinese medicine."

Of course, new scientific evidence gives a different explanation. For example, Tetrahydrocannabinol (THC) lowers body temperature by affecting the hypothalamus.

Cannabis Strains

You might have seen the words "indica," "Sativa," and "hybrid" when you read about marijuana or went to a dispensary. Most people usually put marijuana into one of these three groups.

People think that smoking Indica, which comes from India's Hindu Kush Mountains, calms them. However, Sativa makes you feel more energetic, while the hybrid is a mix of both.

What you want to feel depends on which strain you choose. As was already said, there are many ways to use cannabis as medicine, but some strains are better for some conditions than others.

It's also a good idea to look into the strain's possible side effects. Many of the most common strains, like those listed below, can cause dry mouth, dry eyes, and dizziness. Marijuana could also react badly with other medicines you might be taking. Do not use machinery if you are high on marijuana.

Cannabis Strains and their effects on the Mind, Body, and Soul

Many people have only heard of the two most common strains of cannabis, Indica and Sativa. However, most strains grown today are neither pure indica nor pure Sativa. Hybrids are types of cannabis that are a mix of both Indica and Sativa strains.

Indica marijuana makes people feel calm and relaxed, and its stronger strains can cause "couch lock," which makes people want to lie down and relax for the rest of the high. People with anxiety and muscle spasms often choose Indica strains because they make them feel sleepy.

On the other hand, Sativa cannabis is more energizing

and wakes you up. It is often used to help people focus and get more done, and it is the plant of choice for people who want to ease the symptoms of ADHD or depression.

By mixing different strains of cannabis, growers can make hybrid strains that combine the best parts of their parent strains for a more personalized high. This makes a customized high for people who use cannabis for fun and helps people who use cannabis for medical reasons target and treat specific symptoms.

Improving my mood with cannabis

Everyone knows that marijuana makes you feel good. This has been shown in many kinds of media for a long time. From old stoner movies with Seth Rogen's infectious laugh to pictures of hippies listening to music while sitting on the grass of huge amphitheaters, weed is shown to make everyone feel better.

Calm

Most cannabis strains that help you calm down and relax are dominated by Indica and have a good balance of THC and CBD. Strains with more CBD than THC will help you calm your mind and feel at peace.

Energize

Most high-energy strains are Sativa-dominant strains with THC, CBD, or sometimes both. Strains that give you energy help you fight off tiredness and sleepiness.

Elevate

THC-heavy strains usually work best to make you feel better. Most of the time, THC-dominant strains help lift people out of bad moods and give them more energy and drive. Most THC-dominant strains make you hungry, want to talk to other people, and make you more creative. Most of the time, these strains make people feel happy.

Sleep

Most strains of cannabis that help you sleep are high in Indica. Most people can get a good night's sleep with the help of these sleep-inducing strains. They can help fight insomnia, ease pain, and relax muscles.

Easing my pain with cannabis

The most important thing to remember when it comes to CBD and pain is that not all forms of CBD are the same, just like not all types of pain are the same. CBD products may help some types of pain, but there is no one-size-fits-all solution.

CBD is anti-inflammatory at the cell level, similar to how NSAIDs work. But more research with people is needed to find out how CBD might help treat inflammation in people.

Even so, many studies have shown that cannabis can still improve a person's quality of life and ability to get through the day, even if it doesn't reduce pain. This suggests that cannabis might be an excellent way to deal with the pain rather than a way to get rid of it.

Digestion

When it comes to inflammatory gastrointestinal disorders, preparations that have both THC and CBD seem to help with symptoms the most. This is partly because THC activates CB1 receptors, but CBD and THC synergistically affect CB2 receptors. Studies have shown that the combination helps people with inflammatory bowel disease feel less pain and have fewer bowel movements.

Also, cannabis seems to slow down the emptying of the stomach, the production of gastric acid, and food movement through the digestive tract.

Neurological Disorder

There is much information about how cannabis and its

parts can be used to treat neurological disorders. Cannabis and neurological disorders are a big topic. Most pharmacists probably know that cannabis can be used to treat seizures.

Inconclusive data

Cannabis can help with the symptoms of most diseases that affect the nerves. During her talk, Faulkner talked about the research on multiple sclerosis, Parkinson's disease, and headache disorders, all neurological conditions other than epilepsy.

Source and Supply

To ensure you only get high-quality marijuana, you need to look at more than just the amount of THC and the strain. It's easy to forget that there's more to weed than strain and THC content if you haven't tried it differently and seen how it makes you feel.

If you know what you're doing, buying high-quality marijuana won't be as scary. But first, you need to cover all your bases and learn the common terms you will see when shopping for good cannabis.

How cannabis is used

People often use cannabis to improve their mood, calm down, and feel less stressed. Many say they use cannabis to calm down, relax, relieve health symptoms, and generally feel better.

How much you use is a big part of how safe and responsible your cannabis use is. When you use too much cannabis, you are more likely to have bad side effects and bad things happen in your life. The most significant risks of using cannabis are using it often and using a lot of THC.

A general look at marijuana

Even though many people who use cannabis do it for fun, some need it because it makes them feel better. To use cannabis as medicine, you need to know about the different compounds related to your condition. You also need to know which strains have the compounds you need. There are many different chemicals in marijuana, and each strain has many different compounds.

Since cannabis is legal in some states and countries, many different products have been made, some of which claim to cure certain illnesses. Most of these things have been on sale for less than two years. New things are coming out. Some of these products may not have any CBD, even though the labels say they do. Some things, like heavy metals and solvents, have poisonous parts.

So, if you were waiting for the right time to take advantage of this cannabis chance, that time is now. Download this book and talk to other people about what you've learned.

11

REFERENCES

I would be honored if you would take the time to leave a review)

HTTPS://WWW.SYDNEY.EDU.AU/LAMBERT/MEDICINAL-CANNABIS/HISTORY-OF-CANNABIS.HTML#

https://www.history.com/topics/1980s/just-say-no

https://boardroom.tv/cannabis-weedmaps-social-stigma/

https://www.history.com/topics/crime/history-of-marijuana

https://www.ncbi.nlm.nih.gov/pmc/articles/PMC7605027/

https://thelodgecannabis.com/blog/how-many-cannabis-strains-are-there/

https://www.lexico.com/synonyms/cannabis

https://www.britannica.com/science/marijuana

https://silver-therapeutics.com/cannabis-strains-101/

https://www.healthline.com/health/beginners-guide-to-marijuana-strains

https://www.medicalnewstoday.com/articles/marijuana-strains

https://www.healthline.com/health/cbd-vs-thc

https://silver-therapeutics.com/cannabis-strains-101/

https://silver-therapeutics.com/cannabis-strains-101/

https://www.healthline.com/health/can-you-overdose-on-marijuana

https://www.medicalnewstoday.com/articles/endo cannabinoid#:~

https://www.healthline.com/health/endocannabinoid-system#:~

https://arborswellness.com/blog/what-is-cbd-and-how-is-it-different-from-thc/

https://www.youtube.com/watch?v=oeF6rFN9org

https://www.youtube.com/watch?v=1iIENII-lVo

https://www.webmd.com/pain-management/cbd-thc-difference

https://www.webmd.com/mental-health/addiction/marijuana-use-and-its-effects#:~

https://www.healthline.com/nutrition/cbd-oil-benefits#considerations

https://www.healthline.com/health/cbd-vs-thc

https://jamanetwork.com/journals/jamanetworkopen/fullarticle/2769386

https://link.springer.com/article/10.1007/s00213-021-06047-8

https://www.medicalnewstoday.com/articles/best-cbd-oil-for-anxiety#types

https://adai.uw.edu/pubs/pdf/2017mjanxiety.pdf

https://www.healthline.com/health/marijuana-and-anxiety

https://www.verywellmind.com/marijuana-and-anxiety-1393132

https://www.health.harvard.edu/blog/cbd-for-chronic-pain-the-science-doesnt-match-the-marketing-2020092321003

https://www.medicalnewstoday.com/articles/322051#best-strains

https://patient.practicalpainmanagement.com/treatments/medical-marijuana-pain-what-use-for

https://wayofleaf.com/cannabis/ailments/how-to-use-marijuana-for-pain-relief-explained

https://www.healthgrades.com/right-care/digestive-health/how-cannabis-is-used-to-relieve-digestive-disorders

https://www.frederickhealth.org/news/2021/july/10-signs-of-an-unhealthy-gut/

https://www.leafly.com/strains/lists/condition/gastrointestinal-disorder

https://www.healthgrades.com/right-care/digestive-health/how-cannabis-is-used-to-relieve-digestive-disorders

https://www.ajmc.com/view/cannabis-shown-to-relieve-parkinson-disease-symptoms

https://www.mssociety.org.uk/about-ms/treatments-and-therapies/cannabis#

https://www.mmtcfl.com/muscular-dystrophy/

https://www.ted.com/talks/dr_alan_shackelford_how_medical_marijuana_worked_miracles_for_a_5_year_old

https://www.ncbi.nlm.nih.gov/pmc/articles/PMC6682376/#

https://www.ncbi.nlm.nih.gov/pmc/articles/PMC5938896/

https://leafwell.com/blog/cannabis-functional-neurological-disorders/

https://premierneurologycenter.com/blog/medical-marijuana-for-neurological-conditions/

https://sn.astm.org/?q=features/need-cannabis-stan
dards-mj17.html

https://www.sigmaaldrich.com/ZA/en/products/analyti
cal-chemistry/reference-materials/cannabis-standards

https://www.thrillist.com/eat/nation/how-to-buy-weed-
marijuana-dispensaries-guide

https://www.self.com/story/first-time-in-marijuana-
dispensary-tips

https://www.talentedladiesclub.com/articles/four-things-
to-consider-before-buying-cannabis-products/

https://www.healthline.com/health/reading-a-cbd-label

https://deeprootsharvest.com/how-to-buy-cannabis-
edibles-7-tips-you-need-to-know/

https://sweetjanemag.com/how-to-buy-cannabis-five-
questions-to-ask/

https://www.foodrepublic.com/recipes/so-you-want-to-
make-some-cannabutter/

https://www.tastemade.com/recipes/cannabutter-and-
how-to-cook-with-it

https://greenhealthdocs.com/cooking-with-cannabis-
cannabuter-recipe/

https://www.rollingstone.com/culture/culture-lists/top-
10-marijuana-myths-and-facts-159385/

https://www.webmd.com/connect-to-care/addiction-
treatment-recovery/marijuana/marijuana-addiction-myths

https://www.mhanational.org/sites/default/files/
Cannabis.pdf

https://www.medicalnewstoday.com/articles/marijuana-
gateway-drug

https://www.varsitytutors.com/hotmath/hotmath_help/
topics/correlation-and-causal-relation

https://theconversation.com/cannabis-education-should-aim-to-normalize-not-prevent-safe-and-legal-use-153966